THE FUTURIANS

THE FUTURIANS

THE STORY OF THE SCIENCE
FICTION ''FAMILY'' OF THE 30'S
THAT PRODUCED TODAY'S TOP
SF WRITERS AND EDITORS

DAMON KNIGHT

JOHN DAY
NEW YORK

Designed by Joy Chu

Manufactured in the United States of America

Library of Congress Cataloging in Publication Data

Knight, Damon Francis, 1922-
The Futurians.

1. Futurian Society of New York. 2. Science
fiction, American—History and criticism. 3. Novelists,
American—20th century—Biography. 4. Editors—
United States—Biography. I. Title.
PS374.S35K48 813'.0876 76-30278
ISBN 0-381-98288-2

1 3 5 7 9 10 8 6 4 2

CONTENTS

FOREWORD

The Futurian Society of New York, of which I became a member in 1941, was a group of hungry young science fiction fans and would-be writers which evolved into a sort of subculture: the Futurians had their own communal dwellings, their folklore, songs, and games, even their own mock religion.

Out of this little group came ten novelists, a publisher, two literary agents, four anthologists, and five editors (with some overlapping of roles). Isaac Asimov, Frederik Pohl, Cyril Kornbluth, James Blish, Judith Merril, and Donald A. Wollheim were all members.

Seven marriages and five divorces took place within the group. Like the members of any other large family, the Futurians sometimes found they couldn't stand each other: there were quarrels, feuds, factions, even a few more or less serious murder threats.

In 1945 the group broke up explosively when Wollheim filed suit against seven other members for libel, but for the seven years it lasted it had been something unique and wonderful.

I undertook the writing of this book to try to explain to myself how the Futurian Society came into existence, how it worked, why some of its members succeeded so brilliantly while others so tragically failed. Along the way, I found out things I had never suspected about people I had known for thirty-five years. Understanding them as I now do, I find them more deeply fascinating than ever.

I am grateful for their assistance in preparing this book to Donald and Elsie Wollheim, Frederik Pohl, Isaac Asimov, Robert A. W. Lowndes, Judith Merril, Virginia Kidd, Judith Blish, Larry T. Shaw, Richard Wilson, Rosalind Moore, Jessica Burns, Jack Robins, Joan Michel, Jay Kay Klein, Sid Altus, Richard Wilhelm, Terry Carr, Robert Silverberg, Bernard Skydell, and Kris Knight; to Steve Miller, formerly curator of the science fiction collection of the University of Maryland, Baltimore County Library, and to Binnie Braunstein, the present curator; to Ron Graham of New South Wales and his assistant Cy Hord, who furnished a collection of Futurian wall newspapers; to Howard DeVore, who lent me Futurian magazines and arranged for photographs of covers and illustrations; and to my wise and sympathetic editor, Linda O'Brien.

Cast of Characters
(in the order of their appearance)

Donald A. Wollheim
John B. Michel
Frederik Pohl
Robert W. Lowndes
Cyril Kornbluth
Richard Wilson
Isaac Asimov
Doris Baumgardt ("Doë"; Leslie Perri) [*m.* Pohl; *m.* Wilson]
Rosalind Cohen [*m.* Dockweiler]
Elsie Balter [*m.* Wollheim]
Harry Dockweiler (Dirk Wylie)
Chester Cohen
Jack Gillespie
David A. Kyle
Daniel Burford
Damon Knight
Jessica Gould ("Toni") [*m.* Wilson]
Virginia Kidd [*m.* Emden; *m.* Blish]
Judith Grossman (Merril) [*m.* Zissman; *m.* Pohl]
James Blish
Larry T. Shaw

THE FUTURIANS

"SAVE HUMANITY WITH SCIENCE AND SANITY"

I f Hugo Gernsback had stayed home, everything would have been different. Hugo came to New York City from Luxembourg in 1904, when he was nineteen. He brought with him the model of an experimental battery, an instinct for evading creditors, and a boundless faith in the miracles of modern science. In the next five years he founded a battery manufacturing company, a mail-order radio parts firm, and a radio magazine, *Modern Electrics.*

In *Modern Electrics* and other magazines, beginning about 1911, he published stories of the kind he called "scientific fiction." They were received with such enthusiasm that he began to think of a new magazine entirely devoted to these stories. In 1924 he mailed out a circular asking for subscriptions to a magazine called *Scientifiction.* The response was disappointing; he abandoned the project. Later it occurred to him that the name might have been at fault (although he loved it himself, and used it as a generic term until 1929). In April

1926, without an advance circular, he launched *Amazing Stories*, the world's first science fiction magazine.

Science fiction under other names had been published and read since the 1870s; now, for the first time, it had a vehicle of its own. It was the vehicle that mattered.

Amazing Stories was a large (8½" × 11") magazine, printed on coarse pulp paper, with cover paintings of outlandish scenes in bright primary colors. At first Gernsback reprinted many stories by H. G. Wells and Jules Verne, but when these sources gave out and he began using the work of amateurs, his readers remained loyal. What the readers wanted was not famous names or polished writing, but unearthly landscapes, gigantic machines, colliding meteorites, man-eating plants, rays of red, blue and other colors. Gernsback understood this very well, although in his editorials he beat the drum for the educational and social value of science fiction.

Gernsback in person was unimpressive: short and slight, with a beaky nose; in later years he looked like an elderly macaw. Among the magazines he founded, two, *Sexology* and *Radio Electronics*, are still being published.

The interesting thing about successful inventions is what they do to people's lives. *Amazing Stories* changed hands in 1929, in 1938, and in 1965; it never made a lot of money for anybody, not even Gernsback; but it was a snag in the stream of history, from which a V-shape spread out in dozens and then in hundreds of altered lives. Among these were the lives of Ray Bradbury, John W. Campbell, Jr., Arthur C. Clarke, Robert A. Heinlein, Roger Zelazny, Isaac Asimov, Judith Merril, James Blish, Frederik Pohl, Cyril Kornbluth, and Donald A. Wollheim. The last six were members of the Futurian Society of New York.

One of the things Hugo Gernsback had done was to create a loyal readership, a science fiction fandom in embryo. Around 1930, readers began to discover each other through the letter columns of his magazines. They formed local groups and correspondence clubs; they published amateur journals of various degrees of awfulness, a few printed, the rest hektographed or mimeographed. (The hektograph, now an almost-forgotten device, makes smeary purple copies from a bed of gelatin.)

Gernsback recognized these developments in 1934 when he announced the formation of the Science Fiction League, a grandiose organization with insignia, lapel pins, special stationery, etc. Charters were granted to groups formed for the purpose in New York, Chicago, Philadelphia, Los Angeles and many other cities.

Picture these science fiction fans at eighteen or nineteen— gawky, pimpled, excruciatingly self-conscious—seeking each other out because they have to have somebody to talk to: organizing themselves by mail into the Science Correspondence Club, the International Scientific Association, the Edison Science Correspondence Club, the International Cosmos Science Club. Up late at night, every night, writing ten-page single-spaced stilted wonderful letters to each other about the Secrets of the Universe and the World of Tomorrow! Some of them are lucky enough to find a science fiction club where they can actually meet in person, see each other in the flesh: then the exhilarating discovery that friends can turn into enemies; the joys of indignation!

In Gernsback's Science Fiction League the seeds of contention were already planted. Some of the members were interested only in science fiction itself: they wanted to talk about favorite stories and authors. Others, the true Gernsbackians, believed in science fiction as a means of recruiting

scientists in order to transform the world by technology. Pro-
totypical of this group was William F. Sykora, a professional
chemist, an amateur rocketry experimenter. His embryonic
antagonist was Donald A. Wollheim, a dreamer, a magazine
collector, a would-be writer.

Wollheim had come to science fiction by a curious route.
At the age of five he was a victim of the polio epidemic that
accompanied the epidemic of influenza in 1918-19. He was too
young to remember it, but was told years later that for two or
three months he had been paralyzed on the left side.

Although his recovery was apparently complete, the disease had affected his muscular development and coordination.
He couldn't play ball, because his hand always arrived a frac-
tion of a second too late at the point where the ball had been.
Cut off by this disability from children of his own age, he
retreated into a fantasy world of books and toys.

Wollheim's father, a doctor who specialized in genito-
urinary complaints, owned a four-story brownstone on East
79th Street in Manhattan. Dr. Wollheim's office was on the
second floor; the family used the first and third floors. The
fourth floor was vacant; here young Wollheim was able to lay
out vast armies of toy soldiers and maneuver them for hours.

Wollheim's interest in toy soldiers led him naturally to war
stories in books and magazines. One day in the public library
he stumbled across *The War of the Worlds,* by H. G. Wells. That
was the beginning; then, in 1927, someone gave him a copy of
Amazing Stories. He was thirteen, and he was hooked.

In high school Wollheim was good at science and math,
but he hated the math so much that by the time he got to
college he had forgotten it all. He switched from physics to
literature, then dropped out of school altogether. When he
was twenty he wrote a story called "The Man from Ariel,"
about a denizen of one of the moons of Uranus. The hero

escapes his satellite in a vehicle hurled into space by a gigantic flywheel, crash-lands on Earth, tells his story telepathically to the narrator, and dies. Gernsback published this maiden effort in a magazine called *Wonder Stories* in 1934, but did not pay for it. The amount due was $10.

Surprised and indignant, Wollheim wrote to other *Wonder Stories* authors, found out that some of them had not been paid either, and eventually combined with three or four others to hire a lawyer. Gernsback settled out of court for a total of about $75, of which the lawyer got $10.

The young author was tall, gaunt and serious-looking. He dressed conservatively; when the weather was threatening he wore his rubbers and carried an umbrella. His brown face in repose had a dour and suspicious expression, but when he was amused, his big teeth projected in a goblin grin and he sputtered with laughter.

In 1935 Wollheim wrote another story, "The Space Lens," about the notion that space travelers hundreds of light-years from Earth, using powerful telescopes, could witness historical events—watch Caesar's campaigns in Gaul, for instance. He submitted this one under a pseudonym, "Millard Verne Gordon," using a friend's address. He wanted to find out if Gernsback would publish that one without payment, too. Gernsback did.

Wollheim went down to the early meetings of the Brooklyn Science Fiction League chapter to see what other people thought about all this. There and at other fan gatherings he met three young men who were to be important in his life: John Michel, Frederik Pohl, and Robert Lowndes.

John B. Michel, then eighteen, was slender and slight, well proportioned except for his bandy legs. ("I couldn't catch a pig in an alley," he once wrote.) His dimpled cheeks were pitted with acne scars. He had lost several molars on the upper left side, and his grin was gap-toothed.

Michel was an only child, born in Brooklyn in 1917. His father, a Jew, had converted to Catholicism when he married; his mother was Irish. The father, a dapper little man, had been an actor before he turned to sign painting.

When Michel was nine, his mother contracted tuberculosis of the spine, a painful and crippling disease which destroys the vertebrae one by one, causing a progressive spinal curvature and leading eventually to paralysis and death. In the same year Michel himself fell ill with diphtheria, which left him paralyzed in the right arm and left leg until he was eleven.

Before he recovered from this, he contracted osteomyelitis, a staphylococcus infection which can cause painful ulcers both of soft tissue and bone; it was to keep him in and out of hospitals until penicillin cured him in the forties.

Michel fell behind in school, partly because of this grotesque series of illnesses and partly because of a painful stammer. When he was fourteen he entered a *Wonder Stories* plot contest and won seventh prize—$2.50. A story written from his plot by Raymond Z. Gallun, "The Menace from Mercury," was published under a joint by-line in *Wonder Stories Quarterly,* Summer 1932.

Sometime in the early thirties Michel joined the Young Communist League and became an ardent Marxist—another pivotal event. Through him, Wollheim and others of his group were introduced to Communist doctrines, and several of them also joined the YCL. When he was old enough, Michel became a Party member.

Friedrich Georg Hans Gerhart Erich Otto Heinrich Kurt Pohl shortened his name early in life, first to Fred G. Pohl, Jr., then to Frederik Pohl. Shortly after he entered school he came down with whooping cough; when he recovered and went back, he got scarlet fever, and so on for about a year, during which he spent perhaps ten or twelve days in class. His mother had a teaching certificate: she took him out of school and kept him out until he was twelve. As a consequence of all this absenteeism, and of the family's many changes of address when he was a child, Pohl grew up a lonely bookworm. He does not remember a time when he could not read.

In his teens he was slender: large-boned but very thin, almost emaciated. Like several other Futurians, he had a dental problem, in his case a severe overbite. His hair, skin, and eyes were pale, his voice papery.

When Pohl was in his early teens his parents were separated, then divorced. When he was fifteen Pohl joined the newly organized Brooklyn chapter of the Science Fiction League.

"I got a postcard from somebody named George Gordon Clark saying, 'We're starting a chapter,' so I trotted right down there. And we had one meeting in George Clark's basement, and then a couple of meetings in a classroom in a public school. Johnny and Donald showed up. We published a magazine called *The Brooklyn Reporter,* and Bob Lowndes, who was living in Connecticut, wrote letters to it, which was the first I ever heard of him.

"And that lasted about a year, the Brooklyn chapter. Then we all left and moved over to the East New York Science Fiction League. And the same cast of characters was there. Lowndes turned up at a few meetings. We all knew each other by correspondence, because we were passionate letter-writers.

"The East New York Science Fiction League lasted about a year. Then we went to Willy Sykora's—the International Cosmos Science Club, which was in the process of changing its name to the International Scientific Association. ICSC was a correspondence club, and didn't have any meetings. The ISA had meetings in Sykora's basement, where he had a jar of ten-year-old urine that he was keeping to see what would happen to it. He'd take it out and show it to us and say, 'Now it's ten years, eight months, and three days old. Still looks like piss.'

"Johnny Michel was a trait-dropper, and he used to let me know that he was much more sophisticated than I was in many ways. One of the ways was that he was a member of the YCL. He made it sound kind of interesting, so I said, 'What do you have to do to be a member of the Young Communist League?'

"He said, 'I'll take you to a meeting and you can figure it out for yourself.' So we went to a thing called the Flatbush YCL, which met in a second-floor ballroom on Kings Highway in Brooklyn. And I discovered that they published a mimeographed branch magazine, and that was my main interest—putting out fan magazines—so I joined up, and I edited the *Flatbush YC Yell* for a while. I was the only one in the whole chapter, and especially the only one on the masthead of the magazine, who used his own name. Everybody else had Party names, but I didn't care."

Robert A. W. Lowndes (he added the "A," for "Augustine," when he became an Episcopalian in the sixties) was born in 1916 in Bridgeport, Connecticut. He was a premature child, born with a clubfoot. The foot was partly corrected by surgery when he was an infant, and Lowndes remembers wearing "some sort of special high shoe" when he was small.

His mother died in the influenza epidemic of 1918-19, when he was two and a half. "At that point my father, who was tremendously broken up, sort of disappeared; I was put in the care of various relatives, and for several years, until my father remarried, was shuttled from one to another. As a result, I never felt I really belonged anywhere."

Lowndes grew up awkward and ungainly, with buck teeth that embarrassed him and made his speech difficult. His arches fell when he was in high school, and it was years before he found out about arch supports. He lurched a good deal; it was not safe to walk beside him. He covered his insecurities with an affected aristocratic manner; I think he must have practiced his sneer in front of a mirror. He fell in love with and proposed marriage to nearly every woman he met, some before he met them. He wrote Baudelairean verse and was addicted to the songs of Noel Coward; one, "Parisian Pierrot," he played over and over. Lowndes was good-natured and sensitive, but had so much armor that it was hard to find this out.

After graduating from high school, he went into the Civilian Conservation Corps in Connecticut. In 1936 he attended Stamford Community College for one semester, but had to drop out and return to the CCC.

In 1937, discharged from the Corps, he starved in the YMCA in Stamford for a few months, writing short stories which Pohl tried to sell for him, then got a porter's job at the Greenwich Hospital. When his friends found out he had worked in a hospital, they began calling him "Doc," and the nickname stuck for years.

Lowndes spent the late summer and early fall of 1938 "vagranting" in New York—sleeping in subways. "Now and then Fred would put me up, now and then Johnny or Donald. Some nights I slept on the floor at the YCL headquarters."

I asked him, "How did you eat?"

"Charity," he said. "One time when I hadn't eaten all day, Belknap Long reached into his pocket and pulled out a handful of change. Well, I put one nickel in the subway and went down to Chinatown, and for twenty-five cents I got a huge, magnificent bowl of shrimp chop suey. I've always remembered that, Damon."

For people of Lowndes's generation, the Great Depression was something that had always existed; it was just the way things were. Few were as poor as Lowndes; Wollheim's father, a doctor, was financially secure, but as Wollheim put it, "The problem was psychological. The problem was that you had no future. I mean, you were eighteen, nineteen, and there were absolutely no jobs, no openings, no anything. It was an endless futility—you knew what you wanted to do, but there wasn't a chance in the world."

Having no real prospects, Wollheim and his friends immersed themselves more and more deeply in the worlds of their imagination. Wollheim, Michel, Pohl and Lowndes all wrote amateur fiction and poetry, and published it in their fan magazines. Wollheim and Michel jointly owned a little Kelsey hand press, on which they produced Wollheim's magazine *The Phantagraph;* Pohl had his *Mind of Man,* Lowndes his *Le Vombiteur* and other magazines. Except for *The Phantagraph,* these magazines were all mimeographed; by now every serious fan had at least one broken-down fourth-hand mimeograph which, if carefully treated, would produce at least twice as many copies as it spoiled. The editor cut the stencils himself, ran them off, collated the sheets, stapled the magazines, mailed them to an exchange list of other fan editors and to a few paid subscribers, and waited for the letters of comment which, far more than cash, are the rewards of amateur publishing.

Science fiction fans are a peculiarly close-knit group—much more so than sports or movie fans, for instance. Several informal surveys suggest that they are more intelligent and articulate than the general population, and somewhat less mature. Many fans and ex-fans have a typically foetal appearance. Fans can often tell another fan on sight, and, apparently, so can policemen. In *All Our Yesterdays,* a history of science fiction fandom, Harry Warner writes that on one occasion "a group of Detroit Science Fiction League members were picked up for violating a teenagers' curfew. At the police station, they told the desk sergeant that they had been attending a science fiction club meeting. 'Christ, you look it,' the officer said. 'Go on home.' "

For some reason, fans in the 1930s were noticeably more belligerent on the eastern seaboard than elsewhere. Personal feuds and threats of lawsuits were frequent; alliances formed, broke up, formed again. There was an orgy of club making and breaking. In the fall of 1935, because of Wollheim's public airing of his grievance against Gernsback, and because he, Michel and Sykora were members of the New York chapter of the Science Fiction League while belonging at the same time to Sykora's rival group, Gernsback formally expelled them from the League and dissolved the New York chapter.

In Wollheim's opinion, Gernsback had not forgotten the lawsuit. "That was the original reason for his disliking us; the other reason was that every time they organized an SFL chapter in New York, we would attend its meetings and subvert them into joining the International Scientific Association. And quite honestly, we were conducting warfare against the SFL, and we were expelled for good and sufficient reasons. The Brooklyn chapter didn't survive its contact with us for more than two meetings. We took them all over—we ate up three or four Science Fiction League chapters."

Having vanquished their common enemy, Sykora and Wollheim began to feel suspicious of each other. Sykora was an intensely serious science-hobbyist fan. With his scholarly stoop, his steel-rimmed glasses, his gray skin and drab hair, he looked more like a janitor than what he was, a slightly mad scientist. In the ISA's magazine, *The International Observer,* he published well-researched, rather stodgy and highly technical articles on such subjects as the chemistry of explosives, descriptive astronomy, and home instrument-making. He conducted rocketry experiments, keeping meticulous records, and made films of rockets that fizzed, looped or exploded.

In the fall of 1935, in Long Island, he fired off two rockets fueled with a "secret" powdered explosive of his own composition. One had a steel shell; the other was made of aluminum. Each carried a payload of letters franked with a special rocket mail stamp engraved for the occasion; each cover had a framed cachet in green, reading:

"VIA FIRST AMERICAN ROCKET-FLIGHT—SEP. 22, 1935."

The incident was reported as follows in *Stamps* magazine: "After rising a short distance from the ground the steel rocket motor exploded with a terrific detonation scattering the fragments of the rocket and the covers in all directions. The envelopes were literally shredded to pieces by this terrific explosion. Out of the total of 255 covers only 28 were recovered, and even all of these were torn and mutilated. The balance of the covers were totally destroyed."

Wollheim, who sent me this clipping, gave me his own recollection of the incident. "The rocket flew up about a couple hundred feet and then blew up, scattering letters in all directions, and also putting a hunk of steel through the arm of one bystander, a little boy. Will was arrested because of that and charged with manufacturing and transporting explosives in New York City without a license: he was duly fined. He was later sued by the kid's mother and I think the ISA paid the fine out of the small profits made by the sale of the stamps. In the pit when the rocket went off were Will and myself (my one great claim to rocket fame)—it was only dumb luck that the damn thing didn't go bang when it was touched off. If that had happened, fandom would have gone down a different historical path."

Sykora's second rocket rose somewhat higher than the first before it exploded, and because the frame was aluminum instead of steel, damage to the payload was less; two hundred and thirty-six stamped envelopes were recovered and mailed.

Wollheim was willing enough to take a chance on being shredded in Sykora's rocket experiments, but he felt there was more to life than chemistry.

This doctrinal difference seems trivial now, but Sykora took it with deadly seriousness. "He had a typically paranoid attitude," Wollheim told me in 1975. "I didn't know it at the time, none of us knew—what the hell, we were kids—but it's a classic paranoid thing, this feeling that 'I have a mission, and I can't quite explain it to you common people, but you must have faith in me and follow me.' And, you know, it sounded good. Sykora believed that science fiction was going to lead somehow or other to some great I-don't-know-what. And he had a good precedent for it, because Gernsback was writing the same kind of thing—how science would save the world, and so on. And I remember about the same time Forry Ackerman coined a slogan, 'Save Humanity with Science and Sanity.'

"Anyway, in the course of the ISA's various campaigns against people who didn't believe in Sykora's mighty mission, we reached a high point after the first eastern convention, a really successful convention, held in New York under the auspices of the New York branch of the ISA—the one at which I proposed the idea of having a world convention in thirty-nine. Sykora backed me up and it was all worked out; we had the field to ourselves, the opposition had simply vanished into smoke, those that didn't like us were isolated, and it was great: I mean, Sykora had actually succeeded in gaining *complete control* of the world of eastern fandom.

"And then one Sunday afternoon, about two, we came to Sykora's house for the usual meeting, and as I came down the street I saw Johnny Michel and Fred Pohl and one or two others standing around outside. I said, 'Why don't you go in?' and they said, 'He threw us out.' Sykora had suddenly decided they were all enemies who were conspiring against him. That in leading the ISA toward science fiction rather than science and education, we had diverged beyond his control. And he literally threw out everybody in the New York branch, and dissolved it: I mean it was finished. And Sykora refused to explain. Michel said he spoke to him and he said, 'You understand why, *you* know why.' "

The ousted members later met and elected Wollheim president, vice president and secretary-treasurer of the International Scientific Association, all at once, whereupon he dissolved the organization. This was intended to make Sykora madder than hell, and it did.

Up and down the East Coast, teen-aged fans were clustering together like junkies. One of them was Cyril Kornbluth; he was fifteen when the Futurians discovered him in the Washington Heights Science Fiction League, later known as the Washington Heights Scientifiction Club, the Inter-Fantasy Circle, and finally the Fantasy Circle. Visitors said its activities consisted mainly of "tomfoolery."

Kornbluth said there was a story in his family that one day when a passerby cooed at him in his baby carriage, he announced, "Madam, I am not the child you think me." His parents, like Wollheim's, were nonreligious Jews; Kornbluth didn't find out about dietary laws until one summer at Grossinger's, a famous Jewish resort in the Catskills, when he innocently asked the waitress for ham and eggs.

He had a deep voice, Tartar eyes and a sullen expression. He rarely smiled, and when he did, did not expose his teeth. The reason for this may have been that he never brushed them, and they were green.

The Futurians in their turn had a "mighty mission," to educate science fiction fandom politically. In 1937 Michel wrote a fiery speech, "Mutation or Death," which Wollheim delivered for him at the October science fiction convention in Philadelphia, because Michel's stammer made it impossible for him to speak in public.*

In January 1938, Wollheim, Michel, Frederik Pohl, Harry Dockweiler and Jack Rubinson organized the Committee

---

*During my first interview with Wollheim in the spring of 1975 I told him what I remembered about Michel, ending, "And, of course, he had a terrible stammer." Wollheim looked thoughtful and said, "Funny, I don't remember that."

for the Political Advancement of Science Fiction (CPASF) and began to promote what they called "Michelism," defined as the effort to encourage progressive thinking among science fiction fans. The CPASF published a journal, *Science Fiction Advance.* Michelism for a while was a burning issue in the Fantasy Amateur Press Association, a confederation of fan publishers which Wollheim had organized the previous year.

Others in Wollheim's circle were indifferent or hostile to Communism. David A. Kyle, who lived with his family in Monticello, was brought up as a Republican, and although he enjoyed playing at being a bolshevik—wearing a red hat and marching in the May Day parade—he never took it seriously.

Richard Wilson, who lived in Richmond Hill, also came from a Republican family. He fell in with Wollheim and his group in the late thirties, and he remembers that somebody once took him to a Communist front meeting: "It was the Young American Writers, somewhere in Brooklyn, and I thought this might be an opportunity for me to find out what other writers did—how they made money, and sold articles, and so forth. And my recollection of it is something like a Hitchcock movie: it was a great big hall with a lot of smoke in it, and somebody was standing up at the podium and exhorting us to get out there and either donate our time to Communist magazines, or flyers or handbills or posters, or to write whatever we were writing and give it the *true slant.* And this completely turned me off, because I wanted to write as an individual, not to promote some cause that had nothing to do with me."

In 1937, before the rupture with Sykora, Wollheim had invented a religion called GhuGhuism, and with help from friends had written its sacred book, the Gholy Ghible. Sykora was the Devil; Wollheim was GhuGhu, an entity hatched from the Cosmic Egg; there were Vestal Virgins, whose virginity was perpetually renewed, and so on. Although this was a joke and was taken as such, together with the Michelists' radical manifestoes it helped to stir up rancor in the fan press. The Michelists' chief antagonist, Jack Speer, wrote this in Wilson's *Science Fiction News Letter,* January 28, 1939:

> Short story—by Jack Speer. One day Pohl, Wollheim and Lowndes got converted and became Christians. The evangelist, not knowing them very well, suggested that they go around and apologize to everybody they'd wronged.
> They decided to be GhuGhuists again.

In an earlier issue, Wilson had printed a postcard from a Philadelphia fan named John V. Baltadonis, which will serve to show the depth of the animosity toward Wollheim:

> JOKE COLUMN FOR NEWS LETTER: Joke number one— Wollheim. . . . Joke number two—First pers. "Who was that man I saw you with last night?" Second pers. "That was no man, that was Wollheim! . . ." You're free to use them if you so desire. I'd like every one to read them, so that Daw couldn't say I keep stuff like that under cover. . . . What for? It's too good!

Eventually there was so much acrimony that Wollheim and his group got tired of it and resigned their offices in the Fantasy Amateur Press Association. They continued harassing Sykora, however, whenever an opportunity arose. (Gernsback was no longer the enemy; he had sold *Wonder Stories* to a chain publisher in 1936 and was out of the field.)

In March 1938 the Michelists joined the Queens SFL chapter, of which Sykora was then a member, and when Sykora boycotted the meetings to protest their admission, they had him expelled for nonattendance. Shortly thereafter Leo Margulies, the new editor of *Wonder Stories,* dissolved the chapter.

In August, tired of destroying other people's clubs, Wollheim and his friends decided to create one of their own. They called it the Futurian Science Literary Society. Its first open meeting was held on September 18, 1938.

The first issue of *Amazing Stories*.

Donald A. Wollheim (oil on canvas by Hannes Bok, 1942).

Illustration by Paul

Still more rapidly it revolved, and then, with a click, the metal car detached itself from the centrifuge and shot skyward at the tremendous speed imparted to it.

THE MAN FROM ARIEL

By DONALD A. WOLLHEIM

● This very short story by our new author is surprisingly absorbing for its length. Here is an interplanetary tale of a different kind—a logical one that is realistically related.

After reading this, you will wonder if all those fiery specks that shoot from the heavens and plunge into the ocean or crash into some uninhabited bit of earth are only masses of burning elements.

● It had been a hot and restless night and I slept little. Now, as the dim dawning light suffused my room with its pale glow, I was lying in bed, wide awake. Outside I could see through my open window that the mountainside was blanketed with the usual morning fog that I knew would not rise before a couple of hours had elapsed. Not feeling in the mood to arise, I just lay there and stared at the ceiling in a peaceful sort of daze.

Suddenly, I became aware of a strange sound outside. It was a whistle; very low and hardly audible, seeming to emanate from high in the heavens. It rapidly grew shriller and nearer, and then I heard a muffled crash somewhere on the slopes below. After that it became deathly still.

Wondering what had happened and believing that it probably must have been a meteor, since that was the only explanation that I could think of, I slipped out of bed and hurriedly dressed. Putting on a heavy lumberjacket, for these mountain mornings were cold, I opened the door and went out.

Outside all was grey. The thick, swirling fog hung all around. Objects twenty feet away were practically invisible. I made my way down the path and struck out through the woods towards where the crash had come. In the mist, things had a way of looming up black and terrifying before one, but as the way was familiar to me, I had no trouble. Clearing the trees, I saw before me a long, steeply sloping stretch of bare soil, covered mostly with rocky dirt, strewn here and there with large boulders. This was the site of a big landslide last year, and it had not been grown upon yet. I made my way through the thick atmosphere and managed to find my way down without mishap.

About half-way down, I made out a huge boulder, looming blackly below, just at the limit of my vision. Against this rock could be seen what appeared to be the figure of a leaning man.

"Hello there!" I called out. The figure turned its head toward me and then, raising an arm slowly as if he were very weak, he beckoned to me. Thinking that he was probably injured, I hastened down to help him, and then stopped short with a gasp. For, from the figure's head, about where the eyes should have been, two darkly smouldering red spots peered out at me.

They seemed to catch me and hold me. My will vanished and I stood hypnotized. I was unable to move of my own volition. Slowly, under a will greater than my own, I walked toward him until I could see him clearly, and then stopped.

My mind reeled at what I saw. For this was no man that stood before me, but something alien. Although human of shape, having bulging jointed arms, legs, and torso, he was not flesh and blood. The entire body from head to foot was composed of a brown porous substance of the same consistency as dried mud. His face lacked a nose, mouth, and ears. There were but the two glowing eyes, beneath

THE MENACE FROM MERCURY

By John Michel and Raymond Gallun

Illustration by Paul

Some caged jungle beast, the *Thelon* rushed about her prison furiously attacking the seemingly fragile veil of light that held her in.

Based upon the Seventh Prize Winning Plot of the Interplanetary Plot Contest won by John Michel, 1094 New York Ave., Brooklyn, N. Y.

CLIVE TORRENCE sauntered leisurely along the enclosed promenade deck of the space liner, *Thelon*. His big, well-proportioned body moved forward with a studied, lazy grace. Clive was happy, for he was free. He had been granted a two month's leave from his post as engineer in the iridium mines of Neptune's satellite, and had promptly come sunward, for he was sick of the dark and cold and loneliness of that far-flung outpost of the solar system. He hated the owl-eyed men who had been under his direction. And in return they had hated him, not because he was unnecessarily cruel, but because he was a native of the imperialistic inner planets. On two occasions only the quick use of a ray pistol and a heavy lash had saved him from death at their hands. He could forget that life now—for two months—two months!

Arriving on Earth he had immediately booked passage on the *Thelon*, which was going on a sight-seeing cruise around the sun. His decision was based partly on impulse; Clive liked to give his impulses free rein, for that would aid him in convincing himself that his freedom was real. Another reason was that the *Thelon* was under the command of one Pakoh, an odd little Martian with whom Clive had become intimate during a year of study spent at Oktool, Mars.

Now there was an unmistakable feeling of tension aboard the *Thelon*. The passengers, for the most part college students of Earth, taking their first vacation trip out into space, lined the broad, quartz glass observation bays of the promenade. Their youthful, fun-loving vicacity seemed strangely subdued. Only an occasional low and rather perfunctory laugh at some light joke told of their attempts to remain carefree. Their expectant attention seemed riveted searchingly on the void. True—there was nothing around to see—only unwinking stars, and blackness. However, something definitely unusual *had* been seen, it might appear again.

All that had been learned of it in the brief moment it was visible, was that it was round and large and a... and moved with darting flitting movements. Its as... seemed definitely sinister but this might be only bec... it was a mystery. And there was a rumor around... certain radio messages had been received by the ...

JOHN MICHEL
Who furnished the plot

RAYMOND GALLUN
Who wrote the story

TODAY the university student does not feel his education complete unless he travels to other lands and observes peoples, cities and customs different from our own. Why not then, when interplanetary travel has become a reality, the "interstellar tourist cruise." Young men fresh from schools will taste of the vastness of space, and the far reaches of the sun's domains.

But these youngsters must not expect such cruises to all be picnics. No matter how well explored the sun's planets, there will always be mysterious beings, mysterious forces, and strange events to add the flavor of danger to such interstellar tours.

On the surface of sun-baked Mercury, the nearest and the most eccentric child of the sun, this story is laid. It is prophetic for its vision of what the tourist of the future might expect.

Clive Torrence ... not share the fear ... his young fellow ... sengers, for, not ... out reason, he lo... upon himself a... hardened and ex... ienced adventurer.

His apparen... pointless stroll ha... definite objec... Without haste ... threaded his w... through the moder... ically dressed thr... now and then nod... and smiling to an... dividual with wh... he was already sli... ly acquainted. He c... at last to a short sp... stairway, at the foo... which stood an off... clad in a white ... form. This man, ... Earthman as were a... of the crew, alre... knew of Clive's r... tionship to the *Thel*... captain.

"The Chief's b... wondering when ... would appear, T... rence," he said with ... attempt at lightn... "Go on up. He ... news for you."

"I hope it's ba..." Clive replied with ... unaffected chuckle ... pleasure. He was th... roughly enjoying ... little mystery wh... seemed to have eve... body so baffled.

Ascending the spi... Torrence entered ... airy coolness of ... control room. It ... a place of perfect ... der, and yet of bewildering complexity. Its white wa... tinted softly by the green rays of an illuminator set in ... ceiling, were lined with levers and gauges, and televi... panels that gave views of surrounding space in all di... tions. A few glass globes glowed eerily among spid... mazes of metal cables.

When Clive made his quiet entrance, the tiny Mart...

Top left, Frederik Pohl (sketch by David A. Kyle, published in *The International Observer*). *Above left,* Robert W. Lowndes. *Above right,* John B. Michel (photo by Jack Robins). *Opposite top,* Cyril Kornbluth (photo by Jack Robins). *Opposite bottom,* The Futurians, 1939 (left to right): Cohen, Kornbluth, Lowndes, Wollheim, Michel (photo by Jack Robins).

THE PHANTAGRAPH

FRAGMENTS OF FANTASY

VOL. 7   AUGUST, 1938   J'mil 4 A. Gh   NO. 1

DESCENT

BY ROBERT W. LOWNDES

The sun has fled: with dark malignancy
Great shadows rise and creep, converge and flow
Into one tow'ring, nameless mass they grow,
Impelled by chant of hellish sorcery;

While, on his bier, the dead, mad poet moves;
His red lips writhe; his dark eyes burst aflame;
He draws about his rotting form the same
Robes that he wore to visit alien loves.

They shrink as they behold him standing there:
His livid mouth spews forth obscenities
Which form a sonnet, hideous and dire.

They scream as he descends, now, stair by stair,
For none can hush the son'rous blasphemies
Which sear their souls like necromantic fire.

Top left, First row (right to left): Sykora, Michel, Wollheim; second row: Rubinson, Kubilis, Pohl. *Above right,* Wollheim's magazine *The Phantagraph,* dated by the Ghughuist calendar.

"IT WAS SO HEAVY HE HAD TO SPEND FOUR CENTS IN MAILING IT"

saac Asimov was born in 1920 in Petrovichi, Russia. He was brought to this country by his parents three years later and became a naturalized citizen in 1928. The Asimovs owned a candy store in Brooklyn where the whole family labored. From early childhood Asimov learned to eat quickly so that he could get back to the store and somebody else could come home. To this day he has not been able to break the habit, and in any dinner gathering he is always the first to finish.

When Asimov came to see me in New York in the fall of 1975, he brought with him a black-bound record book, his diary for 1938. It was in that year that he began to keep a diary; he has kept it ever since, and there are now thirty-eight volumes on his shelf.

"But whereas nowadays it's only a literary diary," he said, "in 1938 it contained full details of every baseball game, full details of the Munich crisis, *every day,* what was happening, what speeches were made; how much money my father pulled in that week, and so on. And also *science fiction,* because in 1938 I was just beginning to write science fiction; my first submission was on June 21, 1938, and after that I always put down where I sent stories and when I got rejections, and so on."

On September 6, 1938, a Tuesday, described as clear and cool, Asimov wrote:

> When the mailman arrived this morning he bore with him a large thick envelope which I felt sure was *Thrilling Wonder* sending me my story back; however it turned out only a letter from Jack Rubinson; it was so heavy he had to spend four cents in mailing it.

Rubinson (later Robins) was a science fiction fan who had belonged to the ISA and who remained in the Futurians' orbit for a few years; he was heavy and slow, and frequently opened conversations by asking, "Is it true that . . . ?"

> . . . He had enclosed three copies of a page-long fan magazine. They were fairly interesting. He also gave me a few other fanmags I might obtain; also an offer to start a correspondence with an English fellow. I sent back a four-and-a-half-page answer.

On September 15, Asimov wrote:

> I received a postcard this morning from a Frederik Pohl, who informs me that Jack Rubinson asked him to invite me to a meeting of the Futurians at 730 Nostrand, next Sunday at 2 P.M. . . . I have decided to consent and accept the invitation, after having consulted with Mama and received her OK, and immediately sent off a postcard to that effect. If the meeting turns out to be very interesting, I will join up.

———————

On September 18, after giving the news of the day, Mussolini's speech and so on, he wrote:

> Personal: I attended the first meeting of the Futurians, and boy, did I have a good time. Attending likewise were such famous fans as Don A. Wollman [sic], John Michel, Frederik Pohl, Doc Lowndes. Dick Wilson was also there, but did not join the club as he is not a socially minded fan. Jack Rubinson was also there; altogether there were twelve, including Wilson and myself. We enjoyed a three-hour session of strict parliamentary discipline—you know, motions and amendments, and votes and objections et cetera. Next time we will proceed to business of speeches, debate, etc. Dues are 10¢ a month, with a 25¢ initiation fee, which I paid, of course. I also spent a nickel on a chance, but I lost.
>
> They held the meeting in a sort of hall which is also a Communist Party headquarters at other times. We have an organ which is called the *Science Fiction Advance,* and comes out once every two months. It was put out by another club previously [the CPASF], which has now broken up, and I have the first two copies. I intend to write for [the magazine], but hesitate to put my name to violently radical and probably atheistical articles, so I am wondering if they will allow me to write under a pseudonym.
>
> After the meeting we all went down to an ice cream parlor where they bought $1.90 worth of sodas, banana splits and sandwiches. I didn't get anything though. There I had an uproarious time with Wollheim [now spelled correctly], who has taken a liking to me.

The club's account book lists the following as charter members: John B. Michel, Donald A. Wollheim, Rudolph

Castown (Rudolph *Castown?* Nobody remembers him), Robert
W. Lowndes, Frederik Pohl, Jack Rubinson, Walter Kubilis,
Jack Gillespie, Isaac Asimov, Cyril Kornbluth, and Herbert
Levantman. All but the last two paid their application fee,
twenty-five cents, "in full."

Dues were 25¢ a month for employed members, 10¢ for
the unemployed. In 1938 and early 1939, only Michel, Kubilis
and Wilson were employed.

At the beginning of October, the club treasury showed a
balance of $1.50.

On October 2, after recording that "Papa has a toothache," Asimov wrote:

> I went off to the second meeting of the Futurians. I think
> there was only one person missing from last week. I had
> even more fun than last time, and we discussed, argued
> and objected for about two hours, with the features being
> the discussion of the three science fiction magazines.
> Then we all started playing ping-pong. Lowndes and I
> teamed up and played double matches, and more than
> held our own with the rest, winning about four and losing
> three. After initial awkwardness I performed amazingly,
> considering that I had not held a racquet in almost two
> years.

Lowndes, although he was awkward in appearance and
movement, had been toughened by several years of hard out-
door work in the CCC, and was much stronger than he looked
(see Pohl's later comment about the distances they walked
together).

The Futurians were apparently not much impressed by
Asimov at this time. Pohl remembers him as small, skinny and
pimpled, and says that his conversation did not sparkle; he

seemed to have absorbed a lot of information without thinking much about it. Wollheim says that later on, when he came to visit the Futurians, he often had to be ejected because he was noisy. "After about half an hour we couldn't take him. Dirk [Harry Dockweiler] and myself, or Dick Wilson and Bob Lowndes would simply take him and heave him through the door. We couldn't stand him, you know. You can't really offend Ike, he always came back."*

The third Futurian meeting was held at Jack Gillespie's home near Fort Tryon Park, the highest point in Manhattan. Asimov got out at the wrong subway exit and had to go down "a series of precipices and steps."

> Pohl wasn't there for some obscure reason. [James] Blish, Michel and Wollheim, who were there, want to break up the Futurians and organize it on a much wider basis, including all sorts of persons with a Futurian mind, whatever that is, and taking all the politics out of it. I opposed it like hell, but got nowhere. The meeting broke up at about 5:45 and I went home with Kubilis, who is a six-foot-six guy.

Walter Kubilis (later Kubilius), who appears seldom in this chronicle, is a gentle, soft-spoken Lithuanian-American. Nobody I talked to had anything but good to say of him. Pohl, for instance, calls him "a really sweet person—a decent, intelligent human being."

---

*Asimov does not remember this, and thinks it is not the sort of thing he would be likely to forget. He does remember a time when he brought his sister Minnie over and the Futurians, for a joke, pulled her inside and closed the door, leaving Asimov in the hall. "I got very panicky," he told me. "I had some vague notion that they might do something to her, and I'd never be able to explain it to my parents. And I remember banging at the door very hard, and finally they let me in."

James Blish, then seventeen, lived with his mother in New Jersey; he attended Futurian meetings for a year or so, then went to college and was seen infrequently until 1944.

The fourth meeting was at Dick Wilson's house in Richmond Hill, Long Island, and again Asimov got lost, but by walking fast made it on time. ("Of course, in those days walking wasn't dangerous," he commented.)

Wilson, a tall, spade-jawed young man, had a soft, almost purring voice. In his fan journalism he could be cutting, but in person he was gentle.

You should see the collection Wilson got. About a hundred fifty science fiction magazines all the way back to the large-sizers, maybe even more, plus *Weird Tales, Argosys, Doc Savages* etc., and also over two hundred science fiction novels.

Jack Rubinson says he has a lot of back numbers he's anxious to get rid of, and that they are in good condition. He says he'll sell them two cents apiece, but I don't know if he's serious. I'll be down Saturday night to look them over. I told him about *Amazing.**

On Saturday, a day when "Papa is sick, the cat is sick, and Minnie had her tooth pulled," Asimov went to Rubinson's home and agreed to buy his entire magazine collection for $2.50. He signed a contract to that effect and made a down payment of 50¢. "Mama put up a devil of a kick when she saw them, but I'll get the *Amazing*s and *Wonder*s yet."

---

*"I had just sold my first story," Asimov said. "On October 21, 1938, *Amazing* accepted 'Marooned Off Vesta,' the third story I wrote. So that my fourth meeting of the Futurians was the first one I attended as a professional. And I told them, of course."

The fifth meeting, on November 13, apparently was held in the Flatbush YCL hall again. I take this account from Dick Wilson's *Science Fiction News Letter,* November 26, 1938:

> The Futurian Society's meeting of Nov. 13 featured a debate between Donald A. Wollheim & Isaac Asimov, with Mr Wollheim resolving that the Martians, who landed in New Jersey on Halloween eve, should replace homo sapiens as inhabitants of Earth. Said he: "On October 30, 1938, Orson Welles broadcast 'The War of the Worlds,' which had half America gibbering with terror, believing that horrible Martians, equipped with heat-rays & invulnerability, were laying waste Jersey & New York. Later, coming to its senses, the U.S. reassured itself, calling the Martians figments of Mr Welles' imagination." This is not so, said Mr Wollheim. It is more likely that Mr Welles is a figment of the Martians' imaginations. As a matter of fact, the people of Mars, having lived so many eons longer than Tellurians, naturally have powers denied us. They knew the state the American mind was in, what with war scares and all, and foresaw just what would happen when "The War of the Worlds," which they also knew about, was broadcast. They took advantage of this, landing their spaceships at Grover's Mill while the panic was at its height. (This is borne out by the many persons who *saw* them land.) (See your newspapers.) They immediately went into hiding and are now waiting for the excitement to die down so that they may emerge and take over the world.
>
> Mr Wollheim then gave many reasons for the advisability of such an action. Mr Asimov then spoke, and tho interrupted by raucous voices crying "What about the Martians?" made no mention of them, dwelling on the

development of the Cro-magnon and the tortures of the Inquisition. One may readily see that Mr Wollheim won by a mile.

Asimov's diary mentions this debate but does not say who won, or even which side he took. The diary continues:

> . . . Besides that, I got elected to the executive council. I had a few games of ping-pong, and also practiced a bit on the piano, working out very painstakingly the first three lines of the "Internationale."
>
> When I arrived at the meeting place, no one was there, but soon Wollheim showed up and we dropped in at Pohl's place. His private room is cluttered with maps, Russia and Spain, pictures, Marx, Lenin, Engels, Stalin, Browder [Earl Browder, head of the American Communist Party], and poems. He's a darn good poet.

The next scheduled meeting was snowed out, but the Futurians met again on December 26. Apparently it was discovered at the last moment that the meeting room at 182 Bergen Street was not available.

> The meeting there did not materialize, and we all trooped over to Michel's house. It's a nice one, and I had simply a devil of a time. I smoked two cigarettes.* Doc Lowndes came over. He's here for Christmas. There was the largest

---

*Reading this passage to me in 1975, Asimov said, "Good lord! I would have offered myself up to slow torture as a guarantee that I had never smoked a cigarette. Gee, that's a shocking thing. There's such a thing as going too far in a diary."

gathering of the year, I think, about fifteen to twenty, of which several I had never before seen, including two girls. They raided the icebox, and I cleaned out a nut dish.

This apparently marks the first appearance of women in the Futurian Society—probably Doris Baumgardt and her friend Rosalind Cohen. Pohl remembers that the Futurian Society was the first fan organization he knew of that had any women at all in it, but the proportion was never large. Wollheim says that years later, whenever he and his wife Elsie were in a restaurant and saw a large party with only one or two women in it, they'd tell each other, "There's a typical Futurian bunch."

Frederik Pohl met Doris Baumgardt in high school, persuaded her after six months to attend a Futurian Society meeting, and later married her. She was a tall, cool brunette who looked a little like the Dragon Lady in "Terry and the Pirates." In the Futurians' fan magazines and elsewhere, she signed herself "Leslie Perri"; her friends called her "Doë." In one of Lowndes's magazines, *Le Vombiteur Literaire* (sic), she published the following capsule studies of the Futurians:

> johnny michel is a scoundrel, may he have a hundred semivombic species of progeny, each endowed with a thousand years of vitality undiminished and the power to rejuvenate him with the turn of each century. people who dabble in theoretical breeding, even to go so far as to sponsor it financially . . . find their reward in hell. hey, hey, johnny, cute little devil! damn.

> wollheim is a gnome whose prototype can be found in a brooklyn department store window . . . nodding a

wooden head and rolling large unappreciative eyes in the
general direction of nowhere . . . we like wollheim, also
generally, but think he was born too soon; he anticipated
judgement day by an eternity or two. we think he keeps
secret some sort of religious fervor. he was caught telling a
rosary, calling off paternosters and ave marias with the
assurance of an elevator operator. i am keeping my eye on
catholic wollheim and shall report developments if typewriters can still be smuggled into secret closets. we reserve
a right to temperament as well as safety.

lowndes has arrived, and the bordeaux has been cracked
by a coup de grace rather than a coup d'etat. it is still,
needlessly, christmas day. prosit, swallow and gulp . . . on
with the comedy . . .

pohl is a quietly burning sun, slightly
hidden behind a film of humanity . . . a pity
he hides his light behind such a bushel.
with some nietzsche perhaps and then a little
of something else thrown in . . .
who can say . . . carry on and . . . out.

lowndes only leaves his chateau in
complacency for the thrill of returning to
his own species of solitude. we all have
our own complete silences . . . lowndes
brings warm earth with the roots of
orchids out with him. our only objection
is that he tries to cultivate them in plebeian air.

kornbluth is a man of a second's acquaintanceship.
we are biased in our approval of him. he likes our art

endeavors . . . nevertheless, steeling ourselves to an abstract
observation, kornbluth is a ponderous manifestation of
aesthetic appreciation. a bull with daisy wreaths strung
around his ears . . .

gillespie is a diminutive delectation of diabolical
digressions. we should like to wrap him gently in cotton wadding
and lay him in a small black trunk . . . trap sprung within
in code, of course, would be the only communicative means of
his genius . . . god save his gentle uncrushed head from
the blows of the foul black world.

johnny deserves a word of kindness, a man of obvious genius,
the genius of shielding the spite of a malevolent
mankind from his sensitive soul with a wavering smile
of infinite delicacy.

Considering that this was composed on the typewriter,
under the influence of wine, during a long Christmas afternoon, I think it is remarkably perceptive. Wollheim as a
wooden marionette and Kornbluth as a bull crowned with
daisy wreaths are particularly fine.

On Valentine's Day, 1939, Doris Baumgardt gave a costume
ball. I take this account from *Futurian News,* edited by Michel:
"Present were John B. Michel appearing as a 21st Century
Romeo in beige velvet tunic and scarlet velvet cloak, Leslie
Perri [Baumgardt] as Pirouette in black patent leather panties,

tulle skirt and bodice and hat to match, Frederik Pohl as an
artist in smock and windsor tie, Cyril Kornbluth as a medieval
witch-doctor dispensing love potions in green satin cloak,
green cap and a huge red swimming tube about his middle . . . Robert W. Lowndes portraying a tragic futurist in
streamlined sackcloth and ashes, Rosalind Cohen in dark
green crinoline and many others all garbed brilliantly for the
occasion."

I can't imagine any of the male Futurians either making a
costume or renting one for a party, and it is my guess* that
Baumgardt, perhaps aided by Rosalind Cohen, made them all.

At the meeting of February 26, according to *Science Fiction
News Letter,* "the 'Things to Come' suite and other recorded
fantastic music was played for the edification of the members'
aesthetic sides. Not scheduled were playing same pieces *backwards* & taking of Asimov on thrilling rocket-ride, blindfolded,
with eggbeater, clanking spoons, spacial sound effects. Mr. A.
was also successfully levitated, after involved, highly complicated ritual."

The Futurians' method of levitating someone was to get
him to lie down on a couch or floor, telling him that after a
short time he would rise, "untouched by human hands." Then
they just left him there; when he got tired of this he would get
up, and the Futurians would say, "See?"

In May, *Science Fiction News Letter* reported that "Harry
Dockweiler has on his dressing table a large photograph of
Mrs. Doris (Leslie Perri) Pohl, to which he has attached a plate
swiped from a public telephone, reading 'Temporarily Out of
Service.' "

---

*Confirmed by Lowndes.

This was premature; Pohl and Doris Baumgardt may have given the impression that they were married at this time, but in fact the wedding did not take place until 1940.

At the meeting of March 26, 1939, the minutes show that a visitor, Robert G. Thompson, was commissioned to make an offer of unity to the Queens Science Fiction League, with a joint meeting of the two clubs to be held at a time and place of the QSFL's choosing. At the same meeting, Pohl discussed his plans for an organization called the Futurian Federation of the World, and Asimov offered to pay dues of twenty-five cents every time he sold a story.

At the April 9 meeting, Kornbluth reported that he had attended the latest QSFL meeting and in Thompson's absence had made the unity offer, which had been rejected without discussion by the director, James V. Taurasi. The Futurians were indignant about this, and voted to censure the three leaders of the QSFL, Sykora, Moskowitz and Taurasi.

At this meeting a question was asked about the club's attitude toward the forthcoming World Science Fiction Convention in New York. Wollheim took the chair to reply, "outlining the underhanded and dishonest actions of William Sykora in this regard as well as the dishonorable acts of the editors of the professional magazines." He went on to say that the club had no official attitude toward the convention, and that Wollheim's original committee had withdrawn in order to avoid damaging fandom by holding two conflicting conventions.

Science fiction conventions, which now attract thousands of people, grew from very small beginnings in 1936 when Wollheim proposed an ISA outing to visit the Philadelphia fans. In October Wollheim, Michel, Sykora, Pohl, Kyle, George Hahn and Herbert Goudket carried out this scheme and had such a good time that they decided on a convention in New York in February of the following year.

The 1937 convention was held in Bohemian Hall, Astoria, Long Island and about thirty people came, including a number of professional writers and editors. With this encouragement, the fans started thinking of a much larger convention, to be held in conjunction with the New York World's Fair in 1939. Wollheim was appointed head of a committee to plan for it.

Then came Wollheim's falling out with Sykora, following which the locked-out members of the New York branch of the ISA dissolved the organization. Next the group joined another Sykora club, the Scientific Cinema Club, and managed to disband that.

In May 1938, making common cause with Sam Moskowitz, another old enemy of Wollheim's, Sykora organized a convention in Newark; it was held May 29 at Slovak Sokol Hall, and drew 125 people. The Michelists were present, distributing copies of *The Science Fiction Advance* and a Michel speech which had been rejected by the convention committee: it was called "The Position of Science Correlative to Science Fiction and the Present and Developing International Economic, Political, Social and Cultural Crisis."

The convention now appointed a new committee, headed by Sykora, to plan for the New York convention in 1939, although the old one headed by Wollheim was still in existence. Sykora called two meetings of his committee, but only Sam Moskowitz showed up. Moskowitz, a young man of great energy, took over the direction of the committee from Sykora, and organized a group called New Fandom to sponsor the coming convention. After some public sputtering, the Michelists aban-

doned the field, and in October, after the founding of the
Futurian Society, Wollheim, Michel, Lowndes and Pohl announced that they would resign from all offices in other fan
organizations.

By vigorous campaigning in the fan press and by publishing a large mimeographed magazine of his own, *New Fandom,* Moskowitz achieved wide support for the 1939 convention.

World's Fair officials offered a free hall and a discount of
20 to 30 percent on admissions if purchased in blocks of five
hundred or more, plus a day to be called the Science Fiction
and Boy Scouts of America Day; but the committee, fearing
distractions, turned this down, and the convention was held
July 2-3 in Caravan Hall on East 59th Street in Manhattan.

On the first day of the convention, when Wollheim,
Lowndes, Michel, Kornbluth, Pohl and Gillespie tried to enter,
Taurasi turned them back. Accounts of this episode differ. In
his history of fandom, *The Immortal Storm,* Moskowitz says that
all the Futurians were asked to guarantee good conduct and
that only the excluded six refused. (Wilson, Rubinson, Baumgardt, Asimov, and Kyle were allowed to enter.) Moskowitz
goes on to suggest that the Futurians provoked Taurasi into
excluding them in order to create a cause célèbre. The Futurians deny all this.

Asimov told me, "I wondered whether I'd be allowed in,
but nobody stopped me, because I had no record as a dissident
or something. And I remember Leslie Perri [Doris Baum-
gardt]—she was in there sort of trying to raise the issue of the
six expelled people, and she said something to me when I went
up to the platform; she made some gestures to me, and I took it
to be general pleasure and encouragement—because I remember also that John Campbell was sitting on the aisle, and

when I came up sort of hesitantly, he put his powerful hand on the small of my back and pushed.

"So I got up and muttered something about how I was very pleased to be there, and I was the worst science fiction writer unlynched, and so on, and got off, and then Doris said to me, 'Why didn't you say something about the expelled six?' or whatever they called themselves. That's what her gestures to me had meant, and I hadn't known it. And I felt very confused and inadequate, that I'd had my chance to denounce injustice to my friends, and I hadn't."

Wollheim said about this episode, "Sykora did publish a statement saying that nobody would be excluded. This turned out to be a fake, and we found out from people who were with Sykora that the decision was made a month before that six people would be excluded. And this has been a sore point with me, because Moskowitz wrote it as if we had gotten in, made trouble and been thrown out."

I reminded him, "What he says is that he asked you to give assurances that you wouldn't make any trouble, and you refused."

"Well, why just us?" Wollheim asked. "You know, later on, Moskowitz and I got together after all the feuding had all wound down and compared notes, and exactly the same thing happened to him that happened to us, about six years later. After New Fandom had successfully run the worldcon, and they were on top again, they met a few more times, and then Sykora denounced them as deviationists and threw *them* out.

"Years later, about 1953, I got a phone call from William Sykora; he wanted to come over and talk to me. He showed up at eight o'clock, and we sat and talked for a couple of hours. And he said that he had given a lot of thought to his problem, to things we had done in the past, and he realized he had made a terrifically basic mistake; that he should never have alienated himself from me and Johnny Michel. Because the three of us were the great power combination which would *conquer fandom.* And about the break with us, when he threw us out of the ISA, he said, 'I won't account for it,' he wouldn't explain it, but he thought he had calculated right at that time. And he said what he wanted to do was to get together with Michel and me, and the three of us would reorganize fandom, reorganize the clubs, and go out there and control fandom.

"I said to him, 'Look, Will, in the first place many things have changed, the world has gone on, we've gotten older, fandom is young, and in the second place I don't have any interest in controlling fandom anymore—I don't think anybody could *do* it, I don't know what your motive is—what would you do with it when you *had* it? And in the third place I'm not even talking to Johnny Michel anymore; we broke up three years ago; and I don't have the time to concentrate on becoming an active fan—it means writing letters, you know, twenty letters every night. . . .' And he was simply taken aback: 'I can't believe this, I mean, I don't *believe* it. Of course you'd be interested, I mean, somebody should do it, somebody should, you know, *unite fandom.'*

"Talking with Sam Moskowitz, years later, I found out the same thing happened to him. Sykora left us and went around to Moskowitz, about a week later, with the same proposition. He wanted Moskowitz and Taurasi to rejoin with him. And by that time, of course, Moskowitz was busy with other things, and he didn't trust Sykora for beans. . . . And about ten years after that, he turned up at a Lunacon meeting, out of nowhere, with exactly the same plan. And again you had the impression that for him, it was still 1937."

I wrote to Sykora in the summer of 1975 and asked for an interview, but got no answer. When I phoned him from New York, he gave several polite excuses, and then made it plain that he just didn't want to talk to me about the past. "That's all dead and gone," he said wearily.

"IF HE WANTS TO KILL HIMSELF..."

Muse of the rolling wheels, I have not wooed
Your varied-breasted sisters for awhile,
But aid him that I sing: the gently lewd
Michel, of carven limbs and shattered smile.
Make his task sweet and smooth it in his hand;
Make his pen swift as wings and strong as will;
Let it be frail and slow as tales command.
But may he by your grace be bent, to fill
This volume with what comes to eye or ear . . .
The multiplying wonders of a land.
From city pavements shall the party steer
A lonely, merry way; unto the band
Which dares it, Muse, I ask but that you say,
*"We who remain bless you and hold you dear."**

---

*Lines written by Cyril Kornbluth on the first page of a notebook John Michel bought to take with him when he drove to Chicago with Donald A.

In New York City in 1939 there was no housing shortage, no air pollution, no mugging in Central Park. In that year of our lost innocence, when Mayor Fiorello (the Little Flower) LaGuardia read the funnies over the radio on Sunday mornings, when a subway ride cost a nickel, cigarettes were fifteen cents a pack and California wine cost fifty cents a gallon, Frederik Pohl and Doris Baumgardt decided to get married. They carried this project far enough to rent a house in the Kensington district of Brooklyn and to invite other Futurians to move in and share expenses. Several members accepted: in August Richard Wilson and Harry Dockweiler actually moved in. They called the place "Futurian House." Michel, who had been in the hospital with chronic osteomyelitis, joined them a month or so later.

The Futurians alarmed their neighbors by loud singing of "The Mikado," impromptu fencing exhibitions on the lawn, and so forth. Their printing press and mimeographs also aroused the neighbors' suspicions, along with the stream of odd-looking visitors. Treasury agents descended on the house one night when a guest named George Hahn was there alone. As Hahn told the story, the agents entered with drawn pistols, and he had a sticky half hour before he was able to convince them that the Futurians were just science fiction fans and not counterfeiters.

Pohl and Doris Baumgardt never did move in, and in October, two months after the founding of Futurian House, Pohl informed the others that the wedding had been indefi-

---

Wollheim and Richard Wilson in the summer of 1939. (Michel was so intimidated by this that he never wrote a word in the notebook.)

nitely postponed. All things considered, the owner of the house was glad to cancel the lease and forgive the outstanding rent if the Futurians would just go away.

"And Johnny had his arms and legs in casts from his osteomyelitis," Pohl told me, "pus-y casts, you know, pretty ripe when they were taken off—so as they were leaving, they propped all of Johnny's old casts in the closet."

Wollheim says they also put butter on all the doorknobs. Jack Robins remembers that it was mimeograph ink; that sounds more likely. At any rate, Wollheim told me, "We were very furious with Fred at that point. Of course that was followed immediately by his becoming a successful editor, damn him, which put us in a position where we couldn't throw him out on his neck but had to cater to him. But our feelings were very touchy on the subject."

Having had a taste of riotous communal living, the Futurians went house-hunting and found a fourth-floor apartment at 2574 Bedford Avenue, a few blocks from Michel's father's house. Wollheim, Wilson and Dockweiler moved in immediately, and other Futurians followed. The name they gave the apartment was suggested by the color of its walls—"the Ivory Tower." There were two large living rooms, separated by curtained doors; behind these were a small bedroom, bath, and a tiny kitchen. The Futurians lined the front room and the hall with bookshelves, and filled them with Wollheim's and Wilson's gigantic combined collection of fantasy books and magazines. In the middle room and the back bedroom there were cots and bureaus, typewriters, two mimeographs, the Michel-Wollheim printing press, and not much else.

In October of that year Pohl had applied for a job to Robert O. Erisman, the editor of two new science fiction pulp magazines (neither of which lasted long) called *Marvel Science Stories* and *Dynamic Stories.* Erisman had nothing for him, but suggested that he try Popular Publications. Pohl did, and was hired instantly. The reason was that Popular, under another corporate name, was about to start a new line of low-budget pulps, and they needed editors in a hurry. "They would have hired Mothra or Og, Son of Fire," Pohl said.

Thus, at nineteen, Pohl found himself editor of two new magazines, *Astonishing Stories* and *Super Science Stories.* His starting salary was $10 a week. ("They hired another editor at the same time, and he had to work for three months for nothing before they *raised* him to $10 a week.")

Pohl's base rate for the two magazines was one-half cent a word, half the standard rate of Popular's other magazines; to get enough publishable material, he had to write stories for himself, and he had to get stories from his friends.

At one point, Pohl remembers, he found himself ten thousand words short of the wordage he needed to fill an issue of *Astonishing,* and there was something like $35 left in his budget. Cyril Kornbluth and Dick Wilson volunteered to fill the gap. They wrote a story in alternate sections, taking turns at the typewriter; it was called "Stepsons of Mars"—a Foreign Legion epic transferred to the Martian sands. "Cyril would write a few sections," Wilson told me, "and then I would take it and go on from there, and eventually we got it finished. It was a rather disjointed piece, as you may imagine; and Dirk Wylie [Dockweiler] then took this manuscript and rewrote it. Then it was submitted to Fred, and he edited it further before it was published. And the pen name on it was 'Ivar Towers.' "

During their first year of existence, Pohl's two bimonthly magazines published thirteen stories by active Futurians (and two more by James Blish, who became active later). Four were by Isaac Asimov, two by Pohl, two by Wollheim (one under Lowndes's name), one by Wilson; the rest were collaborations involving Pohl, Kornbluth, Wilson and Dockweiler in various combinations.

Begun as a means of getting into production quickly, these Futurian collaborations became a way of life. The name "Paul Dennis Lavond" was invented for stories written jointly by Pohl, Dockweiler, and Lowndes, although others sometimes used it. It is now impossible to guess what Dockweiler's contribution was. Although a number of stories appeared under his by-line, they were all collaborations or the work of others; as far as I can discover, the only published story which is entirely his work is a trivial piece of fan fiction called "Stuff," originally published in Wollheim's amateur magazine *The Phantagraph.*

A couple of years later, after I had joined the Futurians, I read a rough draft of Kornbluth's and noticed that the characters seemed to keep switching names. I asked Michel about that, and he told me, "That's the way Cyril writes when Dockweiler's going to do the second draft."

Most of these stories appeared under pseudonyms. Pohl writing by himself was "James MacCreigh," or, on occasion, "Dirk Wylie"*; with Kornbluth, he was "S. D. Gottesman" (a name Cyril had appropriated from one of his high-school teachers).

Kornbluth, the youngest of the group, was its most facile

---

*There are a few other examples of this odd practice in science fiction. Eric Frank Russell published a story, "Mechanical Mice," under the name of his friend Maurice G. Hugi, and Katherine MacLean published one, "Syndrome Johnny," under the name of Charles Dye, then her husband. (MacLean told me that her reason was to give Dye's career a boost.)

writer; he could turn out a thousand words an hour. (For some professional writers, three hundred words a day is a good average.) His collaborations with Pohl looked like sketches for much longer works; they were full of universe-spanning voyages, interstellar wars, rays of various colors, etc., as if the author had plotted a series of novels in the tradition of Edward Elmer Smith but could not be bothered to write it in full. The explanation of this is that the writing was Kornbluth's but the plot outlines were Pohl's.

When he published stories on which he had collaborated with Kornbluth, Pohl took sixty percent of the proceeds. Kornbluth was a willing party to this arrangement, but it was one of the things that later made the Futurians resentful of Pohl.

Kornbluth was not a resident of the Tower, being too young to leave home, but he spent all his weekends there. "He would come around Friday afternoon," Wollheim said, "and to pay his rent he would do all the dishes that were piled up from the whole week before—the first thing he would do when he arrived was to roll up his sleeves and do all these dishes." He usually slept on a mattress on the floor of Wilson's and Dockweiler's room.

"Cyril used to come around and astonish us with his knowledge," Wilson told me. "We eventually found out the key to this, that he was reading the encyclopedia. And he was starting with A, of course—was very knowledgeable on the As, Bs and Cs, till we found out his trick. I know that when we were writing 'Stepsons of Mars,' he put in something about the Roman ballista, and I think he had just finished the article on the ballista."

It may be that he never got beyond the Cs. A year or two later he brought to the Futurian Embassy, where I was then living, a manuscript that involved a lot of remarkably authentic-sounding background about Wales. As he stood in the doorway about to leave, I asked him how he had found out all that. *"Encyclopaedia Britannica,* article on coal mining," he said, and closed the door behind him.

On Cyril's birthday the Futurians surprised him at dinner with mashed potatoes prepared beforehand with food coloring, carefully arranged in layers. When he took a helping, under the white surface he found green and red mashed potatoes. Then they poured him a glass of blue milk.

Another time they used Cyril to test a report that it was scientifically impossible to eat a fried egg under red light, because when you broke the yolk, it looked black. Cyril couldn't eat it.

"We had a copy of 'Sing Sing Sing,' the Benny Goodman version," Wilson said, "and Cyril and Jack Gillespie were mad about that. We had a big console phonograph, with doors that opened to put the records in, and as they played that record they kept turning the volume higher, and then moving closer and closer to the machine, until finally they were playing 'Sing Sing Sing' with the volume turned all the way up and their ears up against the wooden doors. That was the original hi-fi."

(Wollheim: "We were not there more than three months when the people below us moved out, after having been there for twenty years.")

In spite of their earnings from Pohl's magazines, the Futurians were so poor that they had to make their own amusements. They played endless word games—"People" (a form of "Twenty Questions") and "Tsohg"—"Ghost" played by spelling words backwards. "Tsohg" has a strategy not unlike that of chess, in which you offer your opponent what seems to be a winning move, then pounce, as in this example:

	Word so far
YOU: T.	T
OPPONENT: N.	NT
YOU: I. (Leading to *tint, mint,* etc.)	INT
OPPONENT: A. (Thinks he has you; this	AINT

leads to *taint, faint,* etc., and seems to
offer no escape by way of a diphthong.)
YOU: (after squirming, looking at the
ceiling, etc.): U.   UAINT
OPPONENT: Oh, shit.   QUAINT

Pohl and Jack Gillespie invented a version of "Tsohg" called "Dzhugashvili" (from the real name of Joseph Stalin), in which each player was allowed to modify the rules whenever his turn came. Pohl, a night-walker, sometimes came in the kitchen window at four A.M. Kornbluth also practiced this trick, swinging down from the roof onto the fire escape four stories above the courtyard.

"I was older than Cyril," Wilson said, "but he was much more sophisticated. One terrible winter's night we were out walking from someplace to someplace else, and I don't know why—I think it was on Flatbush Avenue; we had walked around for a while and it was very wet, very cold and it was snowing. Cyril said, 'We ought to go in and get a drink. Let's go in this bar.' So we did, and he was going to treat me. 'What'll you have?' he said. I hadn't done much drinking, as a matter of fact. But I thought, as long as he was treating, and it was an occasion, I ought to have something a little out of the ordinary, not just a shot and a beer, so I said I would have a Planter's Punch. This was in January, in a snowstorm. And the bartender looked at me strangely, and Cyril said, 'You don't really want a Planter's Punch.' So we each had a shot and a beer."

The Futurians when they drank anything stronger than wine usually drank this deadly combination, also known as a boilermaker. There was a variant in which the whisky, shot glass and all, was dropped into the glass of beer; this was called a Depth Bomb.

Dockweiler, who liked to be thought of as a two-fisted drinker, once went to Macy's and ordered a tantalus, a device which holds several bottles of liquor, usually three, and can be locked to prevent them from being opened. When the tantalus was delivered to the Ivory Tower, Wollheim was there alone: he pocketed one of the keys and gave it to Kornbluth. For a long time Dockweiler was puzzled by the speed with which the liquor level in his tantalus was going down.

Kornbluth later took up a collection, went to a chemical supply house and came back with everything he needed to construct a still, with which the Futurians turned bad wine into even worse brandy.

Kornbluth, Pohl and Gillespie were New York nationalists. "We didn't think the rest of the world amounted to shit," Pohl told me. "Jack used to say things like, 'Let's sing some patriotic songs, like "The Sidewalks of New York." ' We started one group, just the three of us, called 'the Committee for the Advancement of Greater New York, Including Queens, the Bronx, and Staten Island.' And one of the things that we were going to accomplish . . . there are a couple of islands in the East River which are technically part of the Bronx, but by any reasonable standards would be part of Manhattan—I don't know what the islands are anymore—and we were trying to think of some way of getting them to secede, to rejoin the better part of New York City. If you look at a map of the city, you'll see that on the east side of the island, the Bronx begins about seventy-five or a hundred blocks south of where it begins

.ı the west side. And we were planning to demand *lebensraum,* recapture that part of the Bronx, and put it into Manhattan where it belonged. Cyril lived on 217th Street, which on the east side of the island would have been the Bronx, so it was a matter of some personal concern to him."

As we stood on a New Jersey railroad platform waiting for a train to take us back to New York in April 1975, Fred Pohl told me about some odd pastimes of Kornbluth's: he liked to pour a can of lighter fluid into a toilet, then light it and flush the toilet to see the patterns of flame as it went down. Sometimes he would pull out tufts of absorbent cotton and light them; they would then drift flaming through the air. "Did he have a thing about fire?" I asked.

"He had a thing about death and destruction," said Pohl.

Now the Futurian group was beginning to crystallize. Some of the original members who were hangovers from earlier fan clubs dropped out fairly early: one or two others hung on longer but were not much noticed.

The Futurians had begun to recognize themselves as a group of talented would-be writers and editors. Their formal meetings grew more infrequent; the Futurians became an extended family. The new constitution said that the Futurians were in session whenever three or more members were present.

The core members were Wollheim, Michel, Pohl, Kornbluth, Asimov, Wilson, Lowndes, Dockweiler, Chester Cohen, and four women, all of whom later married Futurians: Elsie Balter, Doris Baumgardt, Rosalind Cohen, and Jessica Gould.

Of the male core members, only Asimov ever finished

college; he was the first to drift away from the Futurians, and the only one who became a member of John W. Campbell's group in the early forties. Many of the others did not even finish high school; they were all bright and capable, but they were erratically self-educated. Wilson remembers once asking Pohl how he knew so much, and being told it was from reading Modern Library books. "I think he must have read every Modern Library book there was."

Wollheim was the group's natural leader, not only because he was the oldest but because he loved combat and was a fertile source of plans and stratagems. He, Michel, Lowndes and Pohl formed what Pohl remembers as the "Quadrumvirate" and Lowndes as the "Futurian Politburo." In the articles Lowndes wrote for fan magazines, he presented himself as the most civilized of the Futurians; compared to the inflammatory articles written by Wollheim and Michel, his were reasonable and even conciliatory in tone, but they were written to the Politburo's order.

"I would not be surprised to learn some day, in a scholarly paper, that fluent rhyming is a function of sexual abstinence," Brendan Gill remarked in *Here at the New Yorker.* Lowndes, in his early twenties, was rhyming fluently. Some of his poems were on weird and fantastic themes, influenced by Lovecraft and A. Merritt, but most of them were erotic and romantic. He was looking for love. In the late thirties he carried on long-range courtships of a number of young women, some of whom he had never met. One of these was Mildred Virginia Kidd, then a teen-ager in Catonsville, Maryland; another was Rosalind Cohen of Brooklyn.

"It was a great writing romance," Rosalind told me in 1975. "I still have the poems that he wrote me, I put them in a scrapbook. He was living in Connecticut at that time, living with his grandmother, and they were doing such unheard-of things as eating dandelions out of the lawn. Because when I tell you money was tight, I mean very tight.*

"So he would come down to New York when he could, and either before or after our thing, whatever it was, he went into the CCC camp. 'Cause there just wasn't anything for him.

"Finally Doc decided he was going to come and live in New York, and he wanted to get married. And maybe I was nineteen, maybe he was twenty, I don't know; we weren't much, anyhow. And I got frightened, 'cause I was by no means ready—I have never been ready to get married, ever. So I wrote him back that if he was coming to New York he'd have all sorts of things to take care of, and I was a responsibility that he couldn't handle. Well, I got back a letter from Doc, saying that I was a responsibility that he did not care to live without."

Rosalind jumped to the conclusion that Lowndes meant this as a threat of suicide, and became so alarmed that she ran a fever. "I finally confessed to Doris [Baumgardt] what had happened, and she said to me, 'His life is not your responsibility. If he wants to kill himself, well then, that's up to him.' Then the fever went away, and I got up and went about my business."

Rosalind may have been faintly alarmed earlier by the tone of some of the poems Lowndes sent her. One of them, called "epos," began:

> fat warm scottie bitch with tender eyes
> i hold you in my arms as a child
> and slowly you change into a darkhaired girl
> warm, sweet, and lovely.

---

*If Rosalind had been a country girl, she would have known that young dandelion greens make a good salad. (Lowndes used to pick and sell them for twenty cents a bucket.)

the white smoothness of your belly i stroke
and run my eager hands between your legs
and knead the delicious softness of your close-set breasts.
thus and thus we play
until the languor of my desire takes me from you,
far from the scent-waves of your heavy hair,
from the cushioned warmth of your breasts,
and the hidden springs of your passion
so that no longer can i hear the muted music of your ecstatic cries.

Pohl told me, "He wanted to marry Doris, and he wanted to marry Roz; he really thought he was going to make it with Roz, for quite a while. After Roz married Dirk, she dug out all his love letters and gave them to Doris, who gave them to me, which was a really shitty thing to do."

Lowndes left Connecticut for good in December 1939, and took up residence in the Ivory Tower just before Christmas. The telegram he sent to announce his arrival got there half an hour after he did, and he has never sent another one since.

Elsie Balter, who later married Wollheim, was the daughter of a jeweler. When the stock market crashed in 1929, jewelers and other luxury tradesmen were the first to suffer. "These women who used to buy jewelry, by clipping coupons, you know—that just stopped," she told me.

In the late twenties she was going to Hunter College, taking academic courses. Her father had a bookkeeper who earned $35 a week—it was a lot of money then. Elsie studied bookkeeping at night and took over the job, at $10 a week, until things got so bad that her father couldn't even pay that.

Then she saw an ad in the paper that offered to teach stenography in exchange for work.

"So I thought, I'll try that. And it turned out that it was a lot of fun to be able to make wiggles and get words out of it. So I taught myself typing, and I ended up in a law office. And I liked that very much. All this time I was going to school at night, taking whatever I wanted. I remember one time when I had one dress, and I was so worried about washing it—and I still remember how happy I was, when I washed it and it came out all right.

"I worked for Roz in the law office, and Roz was writing to Doc Lowndes at that time. And I was very jealous, because she had all these lovely friends. So after a whole year she brought me over to the Ivory Tower. And everybody was standing in a semicircle, and at that time I smoked—and, you know, nobody had any money, and I had a job, so I offered the pack around and everybody took a cigarette until I got to Don, and he wouldn't. Then they all took up the chorus, 'I never smoke, for smoking injures the delicate enamel of the teeth, and when that is gone the rest soon follows and can never be replaced.'*

"Oh, and then the next thing I knew, Johnny had called Roz and asked whether I would go out with him. Well, I was not a very popular young lady, and I was thrilled.

"So we took a walk in Central Park. And then I remember we were sitting on a bench somewhere, I think it was in front of the Public Library, and he said to me, if he gave me fifty thousand dollars, would I have a child by him without marrying him?"

I asked Elsie, "Where was he going to get the fifty

---

*"Taine of San Francisco," a character in an early science fiction series by David H. Keller, always recited this formula when he was offered a cigarette.

thousand dollars? If you'd said yes, he would have worked the price down."

"But it sure made an impression on me," she said.

Wollheim put in, "Michel had begun to develop an obsession, from about the Ivory Tower days, that he wanted to be a father. And I'm simply hypothecating, he never would answer this, but I believe somewhere along the line somebody must have told him, some stupid doctor, that he was sterile. And obviously he had an obsessive desire to prove that he wasn't.

"He married three times, and the peculiar thing was, in the first two marriages, both the women had no children—they both claimed to be either sterile or to have had operations. That led in about a year to hysteria on Michel's part, huge fights and things thrown around."

"But his first wife, Annie, moved to California, got married and had two sons," Elsie said.

Wollheim nodded. "So something was wrong somewhere. But then he found this woman who already had a child by her first husband, who had deserted her. And he moved in with her, and she became pregnant right away."

Elsie: "She had twins."

"And he remained with her ever since, and that was the end of that," said Wollheim.

Not quite.

"Dirk Wylie," the name Harry Dockweiler took at Doris Baumgardt's suggestion, fitted him very well. Dockweiler was a big, good-looking man with a red-gold mustache. He wore a trench coat and a hat with a turned-down brim, and carried a flask and a book of poetry with him everywhere. He usually had a cigarette plastered to his lip, with the smoke drifting up under his spectacles. He was trying to live a romantic dream; he wanted to be a writer, I think, in much the same way that he wanted to be a P. C. Wren hero and fight Tuaregs.

He was the inventor of a drink consisting of one half Coca-Cola and one half milk. Wilson calls it a delightful drink. "Dave Kyle and I drink it in his memory from time to time, and we call it the Harry Dockweiler."

Rosalind remembers the trench coat, and the crossed swords over his bed at the Tower. "And of course that was very fascinating to me, a little Brooklyn Jewish girl, what did I know from science fiction writers, or anything?" She was "enraptured" with him at first sight, but didn't think he was interested in her until they went on a group outing in Elsie's father's car.

"Something happened to the car when we got to this lake up in Rockland County, and we finally found a garage to fix it, because we would have been stranded up there. And the repairman wanted somebody to stay with the car so he could be sure we'd come back and pay him. So somehow or other I got named, and Dirk came to my side, and he said, 'Nobody is going to exploit my girl.' That's the first I knew I was his girl. And that was a great and glorious day for me."

It was a terrible day for Lowndes when he found out; for years afterward he could not bear the sight of Dockweiler.

The Futurians came from mixed urban backgrounds, mostly lower middle class. Wollheim's father, a doctor, was the only professional man among their parents. Pohl's father was a machinist, then a stockbroker's clerk, then a wildcat investor; Kornbluth's was a bailiff in a New York City court; Lowndes's an electrician; Dockweiler's a jack-of-all-trades; Chester Cohen's worked in the jewelry industry; Gillespie's was a trucker; Asimov's owned a candy store; Wilson's was a clerk in a steamship company office; Michel's was head of the art department at a Woolworth's in Brooklyn.

Frederik Pohl's father was a visionary entrepreneur, always chasing some new rainbow. Pohl remembers the family moving twenty times in Brooklyn to avoid paying the rent. In *Hell's Cartographers* he wrote:

> Sometimes we lived in luxury hotels. Once or twice we lived nowhere at all, and I found myself thrust on relatives for brief periods (I suppose no more than a week or so, though they seemed terribly long) while my parents tried to locate a landlord trusting enough to take them in.
>
> When I was seven or eight I discovered that . . . it was possible to climb a subway embankment, step gingerly over the charged third rail and emerge on the platform of a BMT station, which meant that by means of carefully learned interchanges I could travel almost anywhere in the city of New York free of charge. Getting back was more problematical unless I happened to have a nickel for the turnstile, but there were ways: an ill-fitting exit I could slip through, or a fence I could climb.

He also hitched rides on the backs of trolleys, and sometimes on private cars. When he got too old for that, he walked. "I remember walking all over with Lowndes and Wollheim, and Michel," he told me. "Most especially Lowndes; he was one of the few people who liked to walk as much as I did, and we would walk twenty miles at a clip. Dirk Wylie and I always did a lot of walking together, because we never had a nickel for the subway, and if we wanted to go anywhere we'd walk—walk from Prospect Park to Times Square and back."

With Cyril Kornbluth, Pohl climbed trees in Prospect Park and "made noises like goony birds." Sometimes they played the string game: the string was imaginary. "We'd stretch it out across the path, and we'd watch people coming up, and they'd feel for it and look at us. . . . For reasons not known to me, we never got killed." They stayed up all night, then went across the park to Isaac Asimov's candy store in the morning and wheedled free malted milks out of Mrs. Asimov, while Cyril made eyes at Isaac's sister Minnie.

Of the inhabitants of the Ivory Tower, only Wilson and Dock-weiler were employed, the latter in a gas station. Chester Cohen, who moved in late in 1939, had been working as a jeweler's apprentice, but quit that job—"a terribly dull job, you know, mass production crap"—and was living on his unemployment insurance. It was $7 a week.

Before he came to live in the Ivory Tower Cohen had a furnished room of his own, where he lived for a while with a girl named Sylvia whom he had met through Pohl. He was trying to keep this a secret, but his good friend Daniel Burford knew about it and told the others. One night when Cohen and Sylvia were in bed, half a dozen Futurians came over, knocked, and when Cohen opened, stood in the doorway solemnly inspecting Sylvia.

Later, when some of the Futurians were needling Pohl about having lost Sylvia to Cohen, Pohl said something mildly insulting and Cohen replied with something positively rude. He is convinced that Pohl has had it in for him ever since.

"And a dirty rotten thing he did to me at the Ivory Tower: He said he was going to put some new sections in the magazine, and he had one that was called 'Missives and Missiles,' so I asked him could I do the heading. So I worked my ass off on it. I think the result was quite adequate; it wasn't brilliant. And I showed it to him and, 'Oh, that's okay,' he said, 'that'll be five

bucks,' or whatever the price was, 'we'll split it fifty-fifty.'* And
I will not tell you what I told him. A hundred years from now if
I was still alive and he was still alive, I'd hate him. And of course
he did that to get back at me for the Sylvia bit."

Kornbluth wrote a poem about Chester and Sylvia; it was
published in Lowndes's *Le Vombiteur* as "Cyril," by Samuel
Gottesman (Kornbluth's pseudonym), but the original title was
the one I give here.

Sylvia and Chester in the Park

Among the gayest things my eye has met
I number one encounter after dark
With Sylvia and Chester in the park,
When birds made quiet noise and grass was wet.
Her hair, I think, was bound in shadowed net
Of moonrise, and in Mazda flaring stark
The man's face slanted forward as to mark
Some challenge, eyes agleam, and jaw firm-set.

I greeted them and broke the little spell;
Graciously then I took my leave once more,
Looking back once to see the two entwined:
A charming sight!
                    I really shouldn't tell
How then I stumbled homeward, slammed the door
And groaned aloud, "The bastards—oh, the swine!"

Cohen was a slender, nervous young man with wavy dark
blond hair and pale blue eyes. His teeth and fingers were

---

*Pohl denies that anything like this ever happened.

stained yellow with nicotine. His interest in the opposite sex was perhaps not unusually high but was abnormally constant.

Cohen's mother died when he was an infant; he was put in the care of a foster mother, whom he learned to love, only to be taken away from her and sent back to his father. He grew up rootless and insecure. His older brother Eugene, who had remained with his father, went through college and became a teacher; the middle brother, Eddie, who was sent to an orphanage, overcame his extreme nervous shyness and became a commercial photographer, later a troubleshooter for a film manufacturer. Chester had a series of low-paying jobs and never settled down to anything.

Wilson remembers that "Chester always wanted to drink black coffee, because black coffee was what writers, men of the world, drank. And I watched him weaning himself. You know, we'd eat at the lunch counter, and they'd give us a little pitcher of milk. So he started lessening the amount of milk: he'd pour in half, and then he'd pour in a quarter the next time; and I was with him when he did the final drop. And thereafter he had it black."

Wilson had a Royal upright, on which Cohen learned to type; he also had filing cabinets full of fan magazines, and about half the books in the Ivory Tower were his. Lowndes told me, "I spent a lot of time when I should have been writing or trying to sell my clients' stories—I took over Fred's agency about that time—going through Dick's fan magazine collection and making up my own from some of his duplicates. In fact, I still have a Michel-bound collection of the *Science Fiction News Letter* which I stole from poor Dick."

Lowndes's principal client was Wollheim, who had a backlog of unpublished stories. Lowndes sold a few of these to Pohl and one or two elsewhere—one to John Campbell for *Un-*

known. Later on he bought some of them himself for *Future Fiction* and for *Science Fiction Quarterly.*

Pohl remembers Lowndes's flat feet and odd appearance. "He had this strange walk, and didn't get along with girls, and deeply resented it, and developed an interest in Decadent poetry, and French Decadent novelists, James Branch Cabell, stuff like that. Lowndes just had to have some god in his universe: either the god was the Communist Party, or Baudelaire, or Wilhelm Reich, or God. One after another, he tried them all."

Wilson remembers giving Lowndes an old black and red Russian-style pajama top. "The pants wore out or something and I threw them away, and he salvaged the top, or I gave it to him, and he wore it as a shirt. This fitted in with his exotic kind of character.

"We smoked Russian cigarettes every once in a while; we'd really splurge and spend twenty-five cents on a box—they were big long things, three quarters filter and one quarter terrible tobacco—because they were exotic. And I guess we had sympathies with the Russians because of the Nazi business. Maybe it was Doc Lowndes who started smoking them because he had this Russian pajama top, and this was part of the mystique."

Jack Gillespie, "the runt of the litter," was full of quirky ideas. Wilson told me about the time Gillespie came over to the Tower and announced he had just bought a new product, a seven-day deodorant. "He came over on a Friday night—he had just applied this stuff—and he was going to spend seven days with us, to test out this product. He wasn't going to change his underwear, or his shirt: he was going to give it a real try. Well, he smelled all right on Friday night, Saturday and Sunday morning. Sunday afternoon, we were spared what might have happened because his mother called him up and said he had to come home because he had school the next day."

Pohl said, "Gillespie and I wrote some plays together, very much influenced by William Saroyan—he made it possible for one to write a play that had neither point nor purpose—first existential playwright, I guess. And we'd think up marvelous lines, and then we'd get to where there was a typewriter, and we couldn't remember them. So it never came to anything. We decided we would operate as a playwriting team, under pen names. His pen name was going to be B. Ames Henderson, and mine was going to be K. Campbell Reed—I have no idea why."

In December 1939, the Futurians sent Will Sykora a Christmas card consisting of a card with a slit in it, through which protruded a finger cut from a rubber glove, with the legend, "Here's something else to screw your friends with." Sykora, who announced (incorrectly) that the card had been mailed from the vicinity of 2574 Bedford Avenue, offered a reward of $25 for conclusive evidence leading to the identification of the miscreants; later he increased it to $50. There were no takers.

The show trials in Moscow had begun in 1936, the public Terror in 1937. Like most American radicals, the Futurians were unperturbed by these events. The Hitler-Stalin pact of August 1939 was harder to swallow, but they managed it for a while. In December, three months after the Germans invaded Poland, the Futurians published a pamphlet written by Lowndes, "Unity, Democracy, Peace," urging American neutrality.

At lunch with Fred Pohl the day after the fall of Paris to the Nazis in May 1940, one of the Futurians offered a toast to the forces of "liberation." Pohl drank the toast, but he thought about it afterward and decided he could no longer be a Communist.

In that year some of the Futurians decided to investigate Technocracy, then a fashionable utopian movement: it advocated the management of the economy along engineering lines, the substitution of labor credits for currency, etc. Wollheim, Michel, Lowndes and Cohen took the Technocracy study course and met the Technocrats' guru, Howard Scott, a large, domineering man whom Lowndes described as having all of John W. Campbell's least likable qualities. "He claimed the Soviets couldn't build a brick shithouse on wheels," Michel said half-admiringly.

"We were Stalinists disguised as Technocrats," Lowndes told me. "We went into it for the purpose of a cover. We became very subdued and wound up as progressive liberals."

This phase did not last long; a year later, when I came to New York, the Futurians were calling Scott a crackpot. (By that time Hitler had attacked the Soviet Union and the embarrassment of his alliance with Stalin was over.)

That summer the Futurians began putting up one-page wall newspapers in the Ivory Tower every few days, each with a different title, e.g., *The Futurian Fanfare, Ivory Tower Nichi-Nichi and Asahi Shimbun, The Ivory Tower Evening Messenger and Futurian Beobachter, The Ivory Tower Associated Daily Bungle and Wool-Gatherer.*

Kornbluth did one entirely in Latin: it was called *Tabula Futuriana.*

Often the newspaper had a motto on either side of the title; the most frequently used (because of intermittent troubles with downstairs tenants over loud music and other sounds) was "THE FLOORS HAVE EARS!" The next most frequent was "SHADDUP, CHESTER!"

During the hot summer of 1940, responding to some bits of doggerel signed "The Mad Poet" published in Futurian fan magazines, I wrote on a postcard:

if the papers are as truthful
as the papers ought to be
if you've really had a heatwave
that drove jerks into the sea
if the heat deaths have amounted
in New York State, to 2
why in the name of Klono
couldn't one of them be you?

I addressed this to "Mad Poet, 2574 Bedford Ave., Brooklyn, N.Y.," and the mail carrier delivered it to the Futurians. (Klono is a god invented by E. E. Smith; I seem to remember that in the "Lensman" series, spacemen swear by Klono's brazen balls, but I must be making that part up.)

Lowndes told me in 1975 that the first two stories published under his name were not his but Wollheim's and Kornbluth's respectively. A partial clue to the reasons behind this is given by the *Ivory Tower Bugle-Gazette and "Daily Argus"*:

Don and Doc are going around with a puzzled look these days. Øred* took Don's "Inhuman Victory" short with the proviso that it be published under Doc's name since the Ø didn't want to repeat authors of Super-Science Briefs. Latest issues of that foul lie sheet *Fantasy-News* allege that Pohl has accepted a SSBrief by Henry Andrew Ackerman, who authored one previously published. The inconsistan-

---

*Pohl signed his letters with a typewriter approximation of the Greek letter Φ.

cy [sic] of a rule as super-flexible as all that leaves the boys
groggy. Fred ought to be ashamed of himself (editorializ-
ing). He won't.

In late June Chester Cohen went back to work; the event was
chronicled as follows in the *Ivory Tower Times-Courier (and
"Ivory Tower Bugle-Gazette"):*

> Chet Cohen, the Tower's tame proletarian, is off the backs
> of the suffering taxpayers insurance bureau. His job re-
> materialized Monday and again the long plaintive cry of "I
> work hard all day and when I come home . . ." rings
> through these ivory walls.

Cohen's burst of industry did not last long; a later wall
newspaper, called simply *It,* has an item headed "Labor":

> Chet Cohen worked one day this week for Johnnie's
> father.

The Ivory Tower Hammer of God & Pillar of Smoke, dated
July 27, 1940, gives a dismal financial report:

> The Treasury and Finances of the Ivory Tower are in
> absolutely abominable state. If the Gas Bill isn't paid by the
> 30th, we will have to cook over cigarette flames. The house
> has been slowly accumulating a deficit due to undue
> generosity in carrying dead wood earlier in the season and
> in piggish indifference and ingratitude on the part of
> those who have often slept over here week-ends or other
> nights. Now nearing the end of our lease, these deficits are

becoming alarming and threatening. Which is to say that any who can afford to, should rush any payment, however small, to the Tower Funds.

The following issue, called *Der Futurianischer Weltansraum und Freiheitsdichtung Beobachter,* makes it clear that it was Wollheim who was putting up the cash to pay bills, and he was worried about getting stuck.

Richard Wilson, Jr., the author of most of the early Ivory Tower wall newspapers, was born in 1920 in Huntington Station, L.I. His father's side of the family was English, his mother's German. Wilson's mother once told him that his grandfather Julius was Jewish; later she denied having said any such thing, but Wilson likes to believe he is one quarter Jewish and the heir of all that culture.

The elder Richard Wilson had been gassed in World War I and later developed tuberculosis; he was in and out of sanatoriums all through young Richard's boyhood. Even when the father was at home, Wilson's parents were estranged and did not live as man and wife.

Wilson was a precocious child; he skipped three grades in elementary school and graduated from high school at fifteen. While he was still in high school he got a Kelsey press as a present and handset the type for his fan magazine *The Atom.*

After high school he enrolled in night classes at Brooklyn College, but flunked both courses—Spanish and intermediate algebra—the first and only semester. Then he went to work at the National City Bank in New York.

In August 1940, while he was living at the Ivory Tower, Wilson decided to quit his bank job. He wrote a resignation letter headed, "Dear Schmuck," but thought better of it and rewrote the letter more formally.

Wilson had been working for the bank as a messenger, "running around the city with a handcuff attached to a wallet, carrying million-dollar checks between banks." Next he took a job at Fairchild Publications, just down the block from the *Daily Worker.* He was hired as a copy boy, but was soon promoted to the copy desk, at $14 a week.

He said, "I learned my trade from Rack Rachmael, the slot man, a Socialist who read the *Call,* and Ben Levine, who sat at the rim of the horseshoe-shaped desk, as I did. Ben was a Communist who went down the street after his Fairchild stint to the *Daily Worker* to work at a second job. Rack and Ben were professional newsmen and politics never intruded on their work at Fairchild. Both sent me often to the unabridged Webster's (2nd ed.) to see for myself the nuances of meaning (expect/anticipate, imply/infer, bring/take/fetch, and scores more which have stuck with me through the years).

"Ben would be reading a book and would ignore the story Rack tossed to him until Rack said, with an eye on the clock, 'For God's sake, Ben.' Ben would put his book down and swiftly copyread the story, tightening it up, substituting the precise word for the approximate one, deleting adjectives. When he was finished, he'd think for a few seconds, then roll a clean sheet into his typewriter and tap out a headline, or a hed and a deck. They'd always fit, down to half a space. I asked once how he did it. He said, 'When you've been in this business as long as I have you don't write heds anymore; you remember them.' "

The chief of the copy desk, Thomas R. Dash, doubled as second-string drama critic for *Women's Wear Daily.* (The first-string critic, Kelcey Allen, later had a prestigious theatre award named for him.) When Dash had tickets to more second-night or off-Broadway plays than he could attend, he gave the extras to Wilson, who, as unofficial third-string critic, reviewed plays by such newcomers as William Saroyan and Horton Foote.

In forty years of talking to each other, science fiction fans have evolved a jargon of their own, sometimes called "fanspeak." Some of it is a kind of acronymic shorthand, e.g., "FIAWOL" (fandom is a way of life) and "FIJAGH" (fandom is just a goddam hobby). "Gafia" (getting away from it all) started out being what a fan did when he was fanning, but evolved to mean a temporary cesation of fannish activity; in this sense it became a verb, "to gafiate."

The first national s.f. convention, in New York in 1939, was christened "the Nycon" by Forrest J Ackerman, who also named the next two: "the Chicon" (Chicago, 1940) and "the Denvention" (Denver, 1941). Subsequent conventions have been named by others in the same spirit until recent times: the 1976 convention in Kansas City was not "the Kancon" or "Kanvention" but "MidAmeriCon"—an abrupt descent into the midwest of the mind.

In the summer of 1940 the Futurians were getting ready to attend the Chicago convention. Kornbluth declared his intention of going to the costume ball as the comic-strip character Alley Oop: "[He] violently contends that if he goes he will go naked, as the cave-men really were. At the most, perhaps an uncured aurochs-hide hung about the shoulders."

Michel built a model of the superweapon AKKA (from Jack Williamson's *Astounding* serial *The Cometeers);* it was made of a rusty nail, a scrap of wire, etc., assembled on a wooden tripod, and could be operated only by a virgin; but at the last moment it was found that it would not fit into the trunk of Elsie's father's car.

Another complaint about Pohl surfaced, in this connection, in *The Ivory Tower Hammer of God & Pillar of Smoke*, August 21, 1940:

> Michel's finances are in very precarious positions, whether he goes may depend to a great deal on the vagaries of the business office of Fictioneers. You see, our Great Benefactor put things off again until the very last minute—he accepted a yarn of Johnny's about six weeks ago, but didn't send the voucher up till today—the check may come through two days before the Chicon—[that is,] three days after John would have left for Chi. . . . The check *may* come through then—or it may wait until later. Also DAW's finances are not too virile—he can make it but it may depend on the debts owed the Tower . . .

Internal evidence suggests that Wollheim was the author of this.

On the evening of August 21 the Futurians held a formal meeting attended by Robert G. Thompson, Hannes Bok, Kenneth Sterling, Vida Jameson (daughter of the s.f. writer Malcolm Jameson), Frank Belknap Long, Mary Gnaedinger and Isaac Asimov. Three illustrations from *Famous Fantastic Mysteries* donated by Gnaedinger were raffled off; Thompson won first prize and took Virgil Finlay's illustration for A. Merritt's "Three Lines of Old French"; Jameson took a Binder drawing, and Bok, probably with a strained smile, accepted a Frank R. Paul.

Bok was a big-chested, well-built man, blond and snub-nosed, with a quiet and somewhat feminine manner. He was

10¢

ASTONISHING
STORIES

HEREDITY
by ISAAC ASIMOV

JAMES MacCREIGH
RALPH MILNE FARLEY

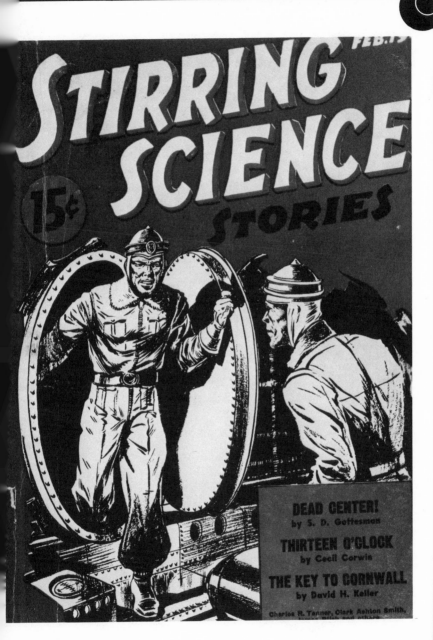

COSMIC STORIES

15¢

MARCH 1941

MECANICA
(Complete Novel of the Future)
by Frank Edward Arnold

Also S. D. Gottesman, Robert W.
Lowndes, Cecil Corwin and others.

FUTURE

DEC. *combined with* **SCIENCE FICTION**

15¢

A COMPLETE
BOOK-LENGTH
NOVEL

AROUND THE
UNIVERSE
by
RAY CUMMINGS

certainly the most talented artist ever to work in science fiction illustration. In black and white, he worked customarily on coquille paper, a textured drawing paper which gives a rich gradation of tones. His forms were sculpturally round, carefully combined into patterns. He knew anatomy and altered it to suit himself; his human figures had bones and muscles that made them more than humanly graceful. When he drew monsters, he often used animal skeletons and superimposed human musculature on them. He had studied with Maxfield Parrish, and many of his oils had the luminous Parrish quality. He specialized in glazes, building up a painting in successive thin washes of different colors, almost like an engraver's separation.

While I was still in Oregon, I wrote to Fred Pohl asking for the original of an illustration of Bok's that I particularly admired, and he sent it to me; I had it for years, and may still have it buried in some box of miscellany. In those days most illustrators surrendered all rights to their work when they sold it, and thousands of original drawings have been lost, destroyed, given away to fans like me or donated to the auctions at science fiction conventions.

Before the Futurians left for Chicago, Wollheim put up the following, headed *The Ivory Tower Defender & Futurian Appeal:*

ATTENTION VISITORS!

Notice:—
DAVE KYLE
ROSALIND COHEN
JACK GILLESPIE

DIRK WYLIE
LESLIE PERRI
BOB STUDLEY

FRED POHL
MYSTERIOUS MAZIE
DICK CRAIN

and whoever else may cast eyes on this including
resident Dick Wilson:—
We can't stop you dear dear people from dropping
around to the Tower during our absence in Chicago and
we don't particularly mind your doing so, but . . . We
respectfully and earnestly request that you remember at
all times that this is not a:—Public Meeting Hall, Camp in
the Wild West, Park Bench, Brothel, Saloon, Salon, or
Business Office.
    This is a HOME.
        Yes, it is.
            We live here.
                It's our home.
    Please try to keep the place in decent order. If things are
in order when you come, see that they are left that way. If
things are in bad order, we would be grateful if you set
them aright.
Please don't let piles of dirty dishes accumulate,
        don't leave lights on, don't make noise,
        don't mess up beds or throw ashes on the floor or
        carpets,
        don't typewrite after midnight, don't use the mimeo
        machines,
        don't make drunken revelries annoying to the
        neighbors.

BEHAVE YOURSELF. SOME PEOPLE HAVE TO LIVE HERE. SO
PLEASE!

Dockweiler, one of those left behind, replied in *The Ivory
Tower Adjutant and Post-Herald,* September 1, 1940:

The belligerant and suspicious attitude of the previous
editor pains us deeply. This snide individual, evidently
judging decent people by his own foul self, has continually
been a source of annoyance to the respectable and all too
small quota of clean-minded and normal folk who ocas-
sionaly (most likely mis-spelt; most likely hell—it is) drop
in for tea and crumpets. He has continually been dictato-
rial, Fascist, and overbearing, trying in the approved style
of Hitler, Mussolini and Stalin to impose his will and
cretinous standards of behavior on others. THIS IS UN-
AMERICAN AND UN-DEMOCRATIC! *IT MUST STOP AT ONCE.*
    PERSONAL NOTES: Wilson is crazy. Gillespie is crazy. Pohl
is crazy. Perri is thorne-smithish. Wylie is mad. Wollheim
is blah. Michel is an ass. Lowndes is a pompous wack.
Cohen is phooey. Asimov is a stinker. Sykora is in jail.
Moskowitz says it's a lie. Taurasi is a pig. Rubinson is a
fumph. LC is a yap. The weather is rainy. We go now.

Wollheim and Elsie Balter, Kornbluth, Lowndes, and
Michel drove to Chicago in Elsie's father's car, a four-door
sedan named Theodore. In *The Futurian Excelsior and Into the
Valley of Death Rode the Fearless Five,* dated August 29 and typed
in transit, they described what happened to them on the way:

Slightly out of somewhere and bearing down upon Cairo,
we came to a fork in the road; we started toward the right.

"Left!" roared three Futurians furiously. The driver turned,* veering Teddy so that for an instant we thought we would go smesh smesh into one of the road signs, but we missed and headed dangerously toward the other side. Again we held our breaths fearing a plunge into a stone wall or whatever it was lay at the extreme right of the road. (Correction: we were going left and people yelled "Right!" Sorry) but again Teddy veered, this time to the left, missing death and desolation. The only trouble was, that in the process, Teddy gasped and rolled over on his right side, causing momentary alarm and a bit of confusion. As a result of such tactics, the windshield, and two windows were left in the road, as well as a generous helping of our oil. Doors were unhinged; things were spilled out (two of our hardboiled eggs casualtied) and a wheel badly bent . . .

Donald just pulled up a huge jagged piece of glass from deep within the frame of the shattered window. Which leaves us with feelings much more affrighted than the actual occurrence itself.

Telling me about this a year later, Michel said that a moment after the car tipped over, Wollheim's long arm came snaking out of the back seat and turned off the ignition.

Lowndes said, "Don hated butter, and cheese. And he didn't drink, didn't smoke. When the car turned over, John Michel swears that as he was getting out of the car, Donald deliberately stepped on a package of cream cheese and squashed it. Then as we sat around outside, Don asked for a cigarette.

---

*The driver, Elsie Wollheim, says it was Michel who grabbed the wheel, causing the car to overturn.

"Friendly people came along and put the car upright; we got in, turned the engine on and it started, so we rode off. Of course, all the windows were broken, the windshield was gone. Next time we pulled in for gas, you should have seen the expression on the attendant's face. . . . The next day it started to rain."

Ye Olde Futurian Armada and Courier, dated August 30, takes up the tale:

About noon today the rain began. . . . We drove into the rain at 35 mph and over, thus bathing the occupants of the front seat and cooling off the occupants in the rear. After three false stops, the rain eventually retired for the day, and we began to dry off. At this time, we hit a 8 or 9 mile detour in Ohio, single lane traffic, through a series of mudholes. . . . Front seaters had to wipe the mud off their faces every time a car passed us.

In Chicago, Kornbluth solemnly polished the imaginary windshield, inside and out.

At the convention Bob Tucker paid a 1¢ bribe to Kornbluth in order to escape being given a hotfoot. Kyle, who had traveled to Chicago with another gang of Futurians, won first prize in the costume ball as Ming the Merciless. Lowndes was second, in a bronze robe with black polka dots, as the Bar Senestro (a character in Flint and Hall's awful old novel, *The Blind Spot).* Kornbluth was the Invisible Man, his head wrapped in bandages.

The Futurians stayed at a YMCA in Chicago. In a nearby bar, at Eighth and Wabash, Lowndes got his foot stuck in a spittoon.

On the way back the Futurians stopped in Indiana to have the car repaired, and found out it would be cheaper to have a whole new chassis put on.

"And we drove back from Indiana," Lowndes said, "with a *two*-door sedan, which we called Tania, naturally. I'll never forget, we came back through some winding passages on the other side of the Hudson. I was getting nervous as we went on this narrow road over these high cliffs going down and down, and every now and then Cyril would whisper in my ear, 'Bang.' "

"...EARS THAT HAD LONG SINCE SHRIVELLED INTO USELESSNESS"

The Futurians were still poor, although Wilson and Dockweiler were working, Wollheim got money from home, and all of them were beginning to earn a little as writers. Chester Cohen was living on unemployment insurance. Rosalind Cohen (no relation), whose family had a catering business, often brought food around to the Tower, and so did Elsie:

"I remember that nobody had any money, and since I was working, I used to bring up groceries all the time, and I got the feeling that I was being put upon but thoroughly, so I wrote them all a letter and said, 'I'm not seeing you for six months until I like myself again.'

"And I remember another incident where Doc Lowndes threatened Johnny with a knife because he thought I ought to go with him, because he wasn't very popular with the ladies. And we were all standing in the doorway, and I turned to Don and said, 'Well, I pick Don.' And I put my arms around him. And of course I had no idea at all that eventually someday we would be married."

"Trapped," said Wollheim complacently.

In 1940, knowing that the draft was not far off, the Futurians felt it would be imprudent to sign another year's lease on the Tower. For the same reason, Wollheim persuaded Dockweiler to resign from the National Guard. Wollheim and Dockweiler went back to their parents' homes. Lowndes, Kornbluth and Cohen took a small apartment on West 103rd Street; they called it "Prime Base."

Kornbluth wrote the last Ivory Tower wall newspaper, *The Ivory Tower Goetterdammerung*, dated September 19, 1940 (with two mottoes above the title, "Ashes to ashes" and "Mene mene tekel"). At the bottom of the page is the following:

> *Hokku in Farewell:*
>   *This ash, this burned match,*
>   *Queen of spades left with tight frown,*
>   *Be happy for us.*
>   *We do not come again.*
>   *We do not come. Ever again.*

In the late thirties and early forties the pulp magazine field was so volatile and the printers were so anxious to keep their presses running that it was possible to go into business as a pulp publisher on a shoestring, with credit advanced by printers or distributors. Most publishers who did so were essentially gamblers who spread themselves as thin as they possibly could, and, like Gernsback, paid authors only as a last resort.

"One day," Wollheim said, "I saw a magazine on the stands

called *Stirring Western-Detective,* a double book. I wrote to this outfit, Albing, and asked them if they wanted to put out a *Stirring Science-Fiction* magazine. They asked me to come over and talk to them.

"It was a father and son, the son in his twenties and the father in his fifties; they were operating out of a desk in the corner of an advertising office, and what they had was credit from one of the news companies [distributors], Kable or one of those outfits, and they said, 'We don't have any capital, but if you can put the magazine together for nothing, we can go up to fifteen bucks for art, and we can do it. If the magazine succeeds, then we'll be able to pay you a regular salary after the third issue.' My attitude was that at least I'd be getting the experience, and something was better than nothing."

With no budget at all for stories, Wollheim was forced to rely on Futurian writers even more heavily than Pohl. The first issue of *Stirring Science Stories* (the publisher had modified the title slightly) contained stories by Kornbluth (as "S. D. Gottesman" and "Cecil Corwin"), Kyle, Blish, Wollheim himself, under his own name and as "Lawrence Woods," Lowndes, David H. Keller, Charles R. Tanner and Clark Ashton Smith. It also included a story of mine called "Resilience" which I had sent to Lowndes. The printers changed a key word in the first sentence, and the story became incomprehensible. The issue appeared in January 1941, when I was going to WPA art school in Salem, Oregon. I was eighteen.

The contents page was divided into two sections, headed "Stirring Science-Fiction" and "Stirring Fantasy-Fiction," separated by a department called "The Vortex." Wollheim had always been a fan of weird and occult fiction, and perhaps he really would have liked to edit a magazine like *Weird Tales;* at any rate, the second section of the magazine was stronger than the first from the beginning.

The stories in the first issue, which appeared among advertisements for "BLEEDING GUMS PYORRHEA TRENCH MOUTH," "SECRETS OF LOVE AND MARRIAGE Daringly Revealed," etc., were unremarkable, with two exceptions, both by Kornbluth: "Dead Center" (Gottesman) and "Thirteen O'Clock" (Corwin).

"Dead Center" is a harebrained adventure starring a superman named Angel MacClure; the villain is a grotesque creation who might have been invented much later by Ian Fleming—"Mr. Sapphire," a 180-year-old man:

> It was the shape of a man—had been once, that is. For it was so terribly old that the ordinary attributes of humanity were gone from its decrepit frame. It could not move, for it was seated with legs crossed and arms folded over the shrivelled breast, these members held in place by padded clamps. The dully-glowing tangle of machinery about it bespoke artificial feeding and digestion; a myriad of tiny silvery pipes entering into its skin must have been man-made perspiration ducts. The eyes were lost behind ponderous lenses and scanning devices, and there was a sort of extended microphone that entered the very mouth of the creature. Sound-grids surrounded it in lieu of ears that had long since shrivelled into uselessness.

Kornbluth wrote this at high speed, with tongue in cheek, and it is full of science fiction neologisms exaggerated just short of parody; like his earlier stories for Pohl, it reads like a sketch for a much longer work, but its vitality saves it.

"Thirteen O'Clock" is a delightful screwball fantasy, full of demons, warlocks, lava nymphs with Brooklyn accents, etc.; it made Kornbluth's reputation and has been reprinted several times. The two stories together gave the magazine its tone and established its rather surprising level of quality.

The illustrations, most of them by Hannes Bok and the talented Denver fan artist Roy Hunt, were exceptionally good. The cover, a black-and-white drawing by Leo Morey with a blue background added, shows a man in an aviator's suit emerging from an airlock whose door obviously does not fit; at $15 (the artist's fee) this was probably overpriced.

Kornbluth continued to dominate the magazine and its companion, *Cosmic Stories,* in succeeding issues, but Lowndes, Michel, Kubilius, Blish, and Wollheim also appeared. Michel's "The Goblins Will Get You" is a deft fantasy about a bunch of insubstantial balloon-headed goblin-creatures who appear at the foot of the narrator's bed and enlist him in their project to take over the world:

> "You fools!" I cried, screaming with laughter. "What could you do with the planet? Enslave it? The rich have done that already. Dissect a billion bodies? Go to our hospitals. They do it every day."

The goblins insist, however, and the narrator realizes that his only chance of saving the world is to trick them into playing poker for it. He stacks the deck, of course. The story ends:

> "Four kings," I said grandly. The world looked good.
> "I have four aces," remarked the other nonchalantly and laid his own hand down.
> You know what that means.

The magazines were discontinued after three issues each; *Stirring* was revived in 1942, in a larger size but with fewer pages; that was not a success either. The Albings went out of business and were heard of no more.

F. Orlin Tremaine, formerly the editor of *Astounding* and

now editor of a new and foredoomed venture called *Comet,* was irritated when he heard that writers were donating stories to Wollheim's magazines, and told Isaac Asimov that anyone who did so ought to be blacklisted. Asimov did not confess that he was one of the culprits, but he asked Wollheim either to publish his story under a pseudonym or else give him a token payment of five dollars. Wollheim sent the check, with a letter which Asimov remembers as "needlessly nasty." All Asimov wanted was the proof of payment, and he says now that he might as well have slipped Wollheim his five dollars back in cash, but at the time that didn't occur to him.

Wollheim told me, "I always maintain that I have a case here, I could sue him for royalties any time his name appears in print—I paid him two and a half dollars for 'Isaac' and two and a half dollars for 'Asimov.' "

Albing also published a love pulp which Doris Baumgardt edited; according to Wollheim, "she practically wrote *Stirring Love* or whatever it was called." According to Wilson, the magazine was called *Movie Love Stories.* "What she would do would be to get stills from the studios, and then she'd get a copy of the script and fictionalize it—turn it into a short story or a novelette. She got Mrs. Gillespie, Jack's mother, to do an astrology column. I think some of us tried to write for her, but it wasn't our thing."

One doubts that Doris did all that for nothing, but whatever the Albings paid her, it probably was not much. At any rate, her magazine perished too.

By now science fiction publishing was in the midst of one of its episodes of lunatic expansion. In 1936 there had been three s.f. magazines; at the end of 1940 there were thirteen. Among these were *Science Fiction, Science Fiction Quarterly,* and *Future*

Fiction, published by Louis Silberkleit's Columbia Publications and edited rather stodgily by Charles D. Hornig, a former editor of *Wonder Stories.*

Silberkleit was dissatisfied with Hornig because it was hard to deal with him at a distance of three thousand miles (Hornig lived in California) and because sales of the magazines were poor. Wollheim found out about this and launched one of his Machiavellian schemes.

Lowndes said, "A batch of pulp magazines appeared on the newsstands, Western, detective, sports, under a new imprint. Donald told me he'd found out these were actually published by Silberkleit. I think the imprint was 'All American.' So he suggested, 'Write a letter to All American, suggesting they bring out a science fiction magazine. And go over all the science fiction magazines and find fault with them, but particularly find fault with *Science Fiction* and *Future Fiction.* And then offer your services to bring out a science fiction magazine.' He had found out what Hornig was getting, and the thing was that I would offer my services at five bucks less. Hornig was getting forty. I offered my services at thirty-five an issue. He said, 'I'll bet you'll get a letter from Silberkleit.' I did. And so early in November 1940, I went down and had an interview with Silberkleit, and when I left, I was the editor of *Future Fiction.*

"It wasn't until many years later that I found out that Silberkleit had tried to get Sam Moskowitz to take the job, earlier, and he declined it because he didn't want to throw Charlie Hornig out of a job. Sam told me, 'I will never strike at a man's job.' Charlie Hornig was not a friend of mine, and so I had no such scruples."

In the first Prime Base newspaper, *The Prime Base Barometer,* dated November 22, 1940, Lowndes gave the contents of his first issue of *Future* as follows: "Kingdom Out of Time" by

S. D. Gottesman; "Martian Guns" by Stanley D. Bell (a reprint from *Wonder Stories*); "The Improbable" by Charles R. Tanner; "The Colossus of Maia" by Donald A. Wollheim; "A Prince of Pluto" by Paul Dennis Lavond; "No Place to Go" by Cecil Corwin; "Within the Bowl" by Basil Wells.

In the same issue he noted that the financial situation was, as usual, dismal: "Checks long due have still to put in their appearance. As a result (a) the Base is a week behind in rent (b) meals have been infrequent and lacking in perspective (c) laundry remains undone (d) outlook on life in general is not as sunny as it might be (e) certain people by the name of F. Orlin Tremaine are being thought nastily of." He recorded the inhabitants' appreciation of "Johnny & Don's company at dinner on Friday nights, when such appearance made the difference as to whether or not our populace ate."

The next issue, *The Prime Base Godhelpus,* dated December 2, revealed that Louis Silberkleit ("Louie the Lug") had not approved the contents of the first issue:

> The Lug, he no like; no unnerstand. But, he says, we are the chosen for his stf* books; only he doesn't trust our judgement inasmuch as we can't use what we'd taken for the 1st stupefying issue. What will happen, GhuGhu only knows. Nothing can be too fantastic in dealing with the Lug, say we.

Lowndes's first issue of *Future,* dated April 1941, appeared without five of the stories he had originally chosen. Three of these rejected stories were by Futurians. Kornbluth's "Kingdom Out of Time," retitled "Dimension of Darkness,"

---

*An abbreviation for "scientifiction."

and his "No Place to Go" (as by Edward J. Bellin) later appeared in *Cosmic Stories;* so did Wollheim's and Lowndes's "The Colossus of Maia."

Meanwhile Dick Wilson and Dave Kyle had taken an apartment on East 61st Street; they called it "the Ravens' Roost." "It had hot water, but no heat," Wilson said. "One of the reasons it was called the Ravens' Roost was that Jack Gillespie came around and fed us every once in a while; so did Dirk Wylie. Dirk would bring things from his mother's kitchen, in bowls, and Jack's father, who was in the trucking business, used to truck Goobers—chocolate-covered peanuts. And every so often a case of Goobers—a hundred and forty-four packages—would fall off the truck somehow, and of course they were damaged goods, and Jack would bring them to us. If we weren't home, he'd go up one more flight to the roof and drop them down onto our fire escape. We'd find them there in the morning, or when we got home.

"Dave was going to art school, and I guess he got an allowance, but he didn't have spending money. We learned to smoke pipes at that time. And we always had a pack of cigarettes, but we smoked them very sparingly. I remember one time we decided to show we were not poor, and we went to call on Alden Norton [then editor of *Super Science*]; we went to the subway and squeezed through the tall turnstile, two for a nickel—and when we got to Norton's office, we grandly offered him a tailor-made cigarette, which he declined.

"We tried baking once, but forgot to put in the yeast, and it turned out to be a thing about an inch thick. It was like a huge petrified mushroom; we used it as a doorstop.

"Another time it was quite cold and we decided to steam-heat the place. We turned on the hot water in the shower and the steam came out into the apartment, and kept coming lower and lower until it was below head level, and we would shout to each other through the fog—which was fine, it was nice and warm, until it began to rain."

In *The Prime Base Hangover,* dated December 17, 1940, Lowndes wrote:

> Last night upon coming home full of Kuttner's* admirable sauterne, we found the following note jammed into our typewriter: "It's unusually well you weren't home. The following paid a long-deferred visit: dirk wylie." Which leaves us wondering how it got in. Through the window or did some traitor loan it a key? We appreciate its calling when we were out and trust it will use similar discretion in the future an it calls again.

Probably Dockweiler did get in through the window: this seems to have been a favorite route. In the following issue, *The Raving Banner,* dated December 26, Michel noted, "Sleep also broken by sound of Lowndes staggering in through window (at 4 a.m. or so)"; and in a later issue there is a report of Dan Burford's unsuccessful attempt to enter the Embassy by way of the transom.

Early in January 1941 Mary G. Byers, a fan from Ohio who had corresponded with several of the Futurians, turned up in town. Asimov and Pohl were the first to meet her and for several days monopolized her company; then she met Michel, who took her to the Davenport Free Theatre; then Wollheim, who brought her around to Prime Base. She looked at

---

*Henry Kuttner lived in New York for several years in the late thirties and early forties; he moved to Los Angeles in 1941 and remained there until his death.

Lowndes and said, "Ugh! Mustache!" whereupon Lowndes shaved his lip.

The next day she called at the Base and found no one awake; she opened a window, picked up some books from the sill and tossed them at Cohen, who was sleeping in the front room. Cohen sat up. "Miss Byers, I presume?" he said.

By this time, it appears, Kornbluth had gone back to his parents' home and the residents of the Base were Lowndes, Cohen, Michel and Daniel Burford. Burford was from Arkansas originally but had been living in Texas. He was foul-mouthed and soft-spoken, an unusual combination. Like one or two other Southerners I have known since, he took such innocent pleasure in his own rascality that he persuaded others to admire it too. He studied art at Cooper Union, and used his (very moderate) skill to make pencil sketches of the utmost obscenity. Burford, Cohen and Charlie Colcord, a ship's radio operator who dropped in whenever he was in town, went on frequent drinking and whoring expeditions together.

Burford was the hero of a confrontation with Sykora in January. Scott Feldman (later Meredith), the director of the Queens Science Fiction League, had issued a blanket invitation to the Futurians to attend the chapter meeting January 5. Burford, who wanted to attend, persuaded Dick Wilson to go with him.

When the two Futurians had been in the meeting hall a few minutes, Sykora walked up to them, followed by Sam Moskowitz and James Taurasi. Sykora told them that Burford was welcome, but Wilson would have to leave. After some argument and a little scuffling, Wilson and Burford agreed to wait outside while the question of their admission was debated. After an hour of speeches on other topics, they got tired of waiting, entered the hall again and took seats on opposite sides of the room.

Presently Wilson was approached by Taurasi, Burford by Sykora, and both Futurians were ordered to leave. When they refused, a shoving contest followed.

"Sykora went over backward, knocking over three chairs and hitting the floor amidst the screams of women present. Moskowitz, slipping up behind Burford, seized his arms, pinning them to his side, rendering him helpless. At this point Sykora arose and grabbed Burford's left ear, twisting it and tearing the skin behind the ear with his nails." (From *Le Vombiteur.*)

Burford broke free and hit Sykora in the chest, knocking him through the doorway into the hall. Sykora got up, went downstairs and returned a few minutes later with the building superintendent and two assistants. He pointed out Wilson and Burford, and asked the superintendent to eject them. The superintendent replied, "You're all going out; this thing has happened before. I told you what would happen if it occurred again." He threw everybody out and closed the hall.

In *All Our Yesterdays,* Harry Warner says that Sykora's wife "ruined the strap of a perfectly good purse when she used it to speed the parting guests."

The treasurer's report in *The Prime Base Snutchsnatcher,* dated "Casa del Famine, January 15, 1941," reads as follows:

The rent is paid until Thursday; we have no cash in the treasury, nor any sinking fund. There is no immediate way in sight of paying another week's rent on time. We have on hand potatoes, kale and salt-pork, onions, a bit of bread, and a small piece of cabbage. There is also tea, coffee, and a little ill-tasting honey. No milk of any kind; no sugar. Our plight in a word is desperate. End of report.

Cohen was alarmed enough to go and get a job as a messenger. The *Snutchsnatcher* reported: "The hours extend from ten in the morning until around five, and the pay is the unbelievable stipend of one eagle, or ten glittering golden dollars, per week. Plus tips. When asked as to whether or not he would file income tax blanks for 1941, Cohen murmured 'foodfoodfoodfoodfood.' It then transpired that, like other inhabitants of the Base, he'd had little or nothing to eat that day."

In *The Prime Base Doodlesackmaster,* dated January 22, 1941, Lowndes reported that Burford and Bob Studley had gone down to Hudson Street, where Mary Byers was staying, to help her move to an apartment on 103rd Street, but had been intercepted by Mary's uncle, come to take her back to Columbus. Michel later said Mary had called him on the phone from a hotel room in which she was being held prisoner. That was the last the Futurians saw of her until July.

The Prime Base Swindlesheet and Hearstologist, dated February 1, 1941, was devoted to a report of a Futurian meeting which coincided with Chester Cohen's twenty-first birthday.

During the meeting, Cyril, Dan, and Chet went out, presumably to accompany Elsie home. There had already been a small bottle of wine consumed. At about 2 AM, the three returned, in a most blotto condition, Kornbluth carrying an almost-empty gallon jug of wine with him.

For a time, the three kept their noses clean, doing no more than singing bawdy songs and horsing around in a good-natured manner. However, when Cohen left the room for urinary purposes, the others followed and started to mess around with the furnace. Lowndes went out to remonstrate with the three, who were patently irresponsible, and was threatened with violence. Since the three were carrying on in a manner likely to result in serious damage to the furnace, Lowndes called the Superintendent.

The three then went out for more drinks. They returned awhile later, in a still more destructive frame of mind, Burford smashing the light bulb in the front room upon entering, and attempting to shatter the bulb in the middle room, too. The three then went out to horse around the furnace again. At this time, they smashed all the bulbs in the hallway, throwing lumps of coal at same. Reentering the room they smashed another bulb, blowing a fuse in the process. Kornbluth, while not engaging in most of the actual sabotage, encouraged and incited Burford and Cohen to engage in same, considering the entire business as a grand old time. He took particular delight in personally destroying some souvenirs of 1941 New Year donated by Elsie.

Early in February Cohen went out to Queens to stay with Elsie and her father awhile; Lowndes, Burford and Michel moved down the street to another apartment, which they dubbed "the Futurian Embassy."

The last Prime Base newspaper was *The Prime Base Swan-song and Protoragnorak* (sic), undated. Again Kornbluth closed it with a piece of verse:

> *lived we many moons*
> *abaft the swinish cafe.*
> *long hoped for decorations*
> *vanished.*
> *over the horizon. over—*
> *and pretty it swirls*
> *down the laminated bowl.*
> *adieu. my dear friends.*

A few weeks earlier Doris Baumgardt had introduced one more woman into the Futurian Society, a plump, flirtatious brunette named Jessica Gould whom Doris had met in an art class at Erasmus Hall.

By this time relations between the two groups of Futurians, Wollheim's and Pohl's factions, had become strained almost to the point of rupture. Lowndes had begun referring to the Pohl faction as "the Dorlists" (a portmanteau word, from *Doris* and Rosa*lind*). According to him, Wollheim felt the two women were a pernicious bourgeois influence, and he was alarmed about their deviationism in very much the same way that Wollheim's had alarmed Sykora.

In fact, Pohl, Dockweiler and Doris Baumgardt had all known each other since high school; when Pohl and Doris were married in 1940 and took up residence in a downtown housing development called Knickerbocker Village, they formed the nucleus of a natural social group.

Relations between the Embassy Futurians and the "Dorlists" were not improved when Jessica Gould came to the Embassy by invitation, followed in about an hour by Wilson, who took her out for a drink and never brought her back. "The evening then proceeded without the Dorlists. Reliable sources indicate that Toni [Jessica] is not a Dorlist except when in with the company of same boll in the weevil, we mean weevils in the boll of the glorious Futurian movement. As for Wilson: we *know* him." (From *The Futurian Causerie,* February 26, 1941.)

By March finances had improved a little: Burford was getting unemployment compensation and selling a few (bloody awful) illustrations to Lowndes and others. Bills were paid, and there was even a little surplus.

In *Futurian Carbine,* dated March 9, 1941, Lowndes reported that Kyle and Dockweiler had left for Monticello to work for a new daily Sullivan County newspaper owned by

Kyle's brother Arthur. He also noted: "Donald is reading the first 20,000 of a marathon of wordage from Cyril. Cyril has to get in 60,000 acceptable woids by Apr 13 or DAW will not bless his proposed trip to California. We saw the first 20,000 and, while not wanting to stick our neck out, we are inclined to suspect that it won't all be found acceptable."

Earlier that year, Cohen had fallen in love with Elsie; he was boarding in her house and working for her father. "And we were gonna get married, and instead— The job was terrible, nothing much to do, a makework thing . . . Cyril got this idea of taking a bus trip to California. So he talked me into it. *Greyhound bus all the way.* Oh, it was a ghastly trip. I got so goddamn constipated. I was afraid! who could take the time? the bus would leave without me. They told us, if we weren't there on time, they'd leave. When I got to L.A., was I full of shit . . ."

While all this was going on in New York, that fiery crucible, I was a schoolboy in Hood River, Oregon. Both my parents were schoolteachers; I was their only child. I grew up mentally precocious and physically backward; in my high school graduating class I looked like a fourteen-year-old who had got in by mistake.

I discovered *Amazing Stories* in the fall of 1933, when I was eleven; then *Wonder*, and a year or so later *Astounding;* then I found the secondhand bookstores in Portland, with their shelves piled high with huge old *Wonder*s and *Amazing*s.

In one of his short stories, "We Also Walk Dogs," Robert A. Heinlein says of a character's first experience of beauty: "It shook him and hurt him, like the first trembling intensity of sex."

Christ! Beauty was not in it, or sex either—I knew them both, and they were pitiful, pale things in comparison. *Battle-*

*ships hanging upside down over New York! Men in radio tubes being
zapped by electricity! Robots carrying off pretty girls in Antarctica!*
Here was the pure quill, the essential jolt, so powerful that if
my parents had understood what it was they would have
stopped my allowance, painted my eyeglasses black to keep me
from reading such stuff.

I went through all the stages of the proto-fan, recapitulat-
ing Wollheim's phylogeny. In Fred Pohl's magazines I found
lists of fanzines, subscribed to several, and in this way got into
correspondence with a number of fans, including Lowndes,
who kindly offered to look at some stories I had written. In
1940 I produced two issues of a fan magazine of my own called
Snide, one while I was still in high school and the other, with
the cooperation of a fan named Bill Evans, while I was studying
at the WPA Art Center in Salem. *Snide,* I realized later, was my
passport out of the Pacific Northwest. It so impressed the
Futurians that they fell upon Lowndes for writing a lukewarm
review of it in *Le Vombiteur,* and in the next issue he dutifully
published their comments, as follows:

> "Snide is the floating kidney of the stf. move-
> ment."—Michel.
> "Astounding? Amazing? Astonishing? Thrilling? Star-
> tling? Weird? NO! Snide!"—Wollheim.
> "God bless Damon Knight for absolutely the best single
> piece of work I have ever seen produced in
> fandom."—Kornbluth.
> "Snide? I didn't read it."—Cohen.

How the idea of my going to New York came up I don't
remember, but it was somehow decided that I would meet the
Futurians at the convention in Denver and go back with them
to live at the Embassy. My parents fell in with this scheme with

what I thought was surprising alacrity; now I have grown sons of my own, and I know better.

Chester Cohen said about our first meeting: "We were standing around in a crowded hall when I suddenly looked up, and here came a tall, very, very skinny young man, followed by two older people. And the skinny young man came walking up the aisle and bouncing on his toes, the funniest sight I've ever seen. And he wasn't being overjoyed or anything, that was the way he walked. I said, 'Hey, look—that's got to be Damon Knight.' And it was. A country yokel, just what we expected."

The Futurians stood and looked at me, and I looked at them. They were all shapes and sizes. Cohen's hollow-cheeked face might have been handsome except for his low, somewhat receding forehead. He had a blond beard, grown for the occasion. (He appeared at the costume ball as Nehemiah Scudder, the prophet in Heinlein's "If This Goes On—.") Wollheim, dressed in brown, was knob-jointed and awkward; he had a big nose and teeth like a picket fence. Kornbluth was short and pudgy, pasty-faced, Michel bowlegged and balding. Lowndes was portly, with an aquiline nose and a purse-lipped superior smile.

During the costume ball, at which I unwisely appeared in green pajamas as "John Star," the hero of Jack Williamson's *Legion of Space,* Kornbluth said in a stage whisper, "I know it's supposed to be John Star, but who *is* she?"

Later I came to like Kornbluth better than any other Futurian and better than most human beings, but you can judge how I reacted to this remark at the time by the fact that I have remembered it for thirty-four years.

In *Hell's Cartographers* I gave a brief account of our trip to New York from Denver:

After the convention we divided into two groups; Kornbluth, who had been on a trip to Los Angeles with Cohen, got into one car with Wollheim, Michel and me, leaving Chet to go home with Lowndes. "I've seen a lot of Chester Cohen," Cyril said. We were traveling by "wildcat bus"—sharing expenses with a good-natured man named Jack Inskeep who was driving to Cleveland. On the way, Wollheim expanded on an idea of his that the surface of the earth was composed of strips of solid material about two miles across, with roads running down the middle, the rest being hollow. Kornbluth played up to this, thinking of feeble objections which Wollheim demolished one by one.

I also remember that Cyril casually used the word "coitus," and I said, "What's that?" There was an uncomfortable silence until I said, "Oh." I had never heard the word spoken, and didn't know how it was pronounced.

In Hill City, Kansas, the car broke down. Hill City was a slight rise in the road, not more than a foot and a half in elevation. The whole town could have been covered by a single good-sized aircraft hangar. The garage where the car was worked on had a calendar on the wall depicting a bosomy young woman who was not Rita Hayworth, although that was the name printed under the picture.

Cyril made some comment about her "knockers"—I had never heard that word, either.

The one movie theater was upstairs in a ramshackle building, reached by an outside stairway; locusts leaped in the tall weeds nearby. Down a side street, we came upon a house behind a white picket fence; in the lawn was a neat sign that read: "Dr.————, Physian and Surgon."

Near Columbus, our driver obligingly stopped so that Cyril could meet his girl, Mary Byers, who lived on a farm with several fierce uncles. We went to a bar, and Inskeep played the pinball machines while Cyril and Mary stared into each other's eyes. In Cleveland he left us and Wollheim took a train, while the rest of us went on by bus.

Evidently Cyril and Mary had met and been attracted to each other on her previous trip to New York, although the record does not say so; the chronicler, Lowndes, may not have known about it. About the bus trip, what I chiefly remember is that we were sitting on the long seat at the rear, and Michel and Kornbluth were bothered by fumes from the engine. Michel wanted me to complain to the driver: "Tell him we're two sick boys," he said petulantly.

In memory I reenter the Embassy—climb the stairs, round and round, then along the hall, open the door, and I am in the kitchen. In these railroad apartments, the kitchen is always the first room. The ceilings are high. The kitchen is painted a peculiarly dull and dingy white, and looks shabbier than the rest of the apartment. I don't know why this should have been so, unless the lease required the landlord to repaint the other rooms oftener. And I don't know why they were always that almost-white color.

To my left are the sink and the bathtub, covered but not disguised (its clawed feet are visible below) by an enameled drainboard. Straight ahead is a kitchen table of enameled metal; behind it is a window opening on an airshaft. The floor is worn linoleum. The only decoration is a calendar on the wall.

To the left, past the bathtub, is a long vista of open doorways. No one is here. I walk through the first doorway, past the bathroom on the right, the closet on the left where my pornographic magazines are stored in a cardboard carton, beside a pile of Communist pamphlets. The next room is the guest room—nothing in it but a folding metal cot covered with a worn gray blanket. It has no window; the only light is a bare bulb hanging from the ceiling. All the rooms except the kitchen have floors of bare varnished wood.

The next is Johnny Michel's bedroom, cot, wardrobe, bureau, and a dark green footlocker, all neat and clean. Then my room, cot, battered bureau.*

Then the living room, where Lowndes's bed is in an alcove to the left. This is the largest room, airy and bright: it has bow windows looking out on the street four stories below. A card table to my right, with a typewriter on it; a stand nearby with a small phonograph, Lowndes's—it has the kind of turntable that can revolve in either direction, and it has steel needles, or perhaps Lowndes is experimenting with cactus. On the wall behind the table is a cover painting by Hannes Bok: it shows a creature like a ray, with many tentacles, ascending and drawing after it two hypnotized-looking young people, a man and a woman. It is painted on illustration board, partly in oil, partly in tempera, and the tempera is flaking.

How can I explain how happy I am to be here?

One morning I was up before the rest. I looked out one of the windows and leaned over to see the bluish rain-washed street, empty except for two boys playing stickball. Sunlight

---

*It was in this bureau, used to store other people's possessions, that I once found a long poem by Cyril, written in the style of Edgar Guest, which ended: "Emulate the idiot who eats his own shit—*it's delicious!*"

flooded the living room: thinking of the buildings, the bridges, the pure sky beyond, I felt such ecstasy at being alive, here, in New York, that I could express it only by picking up a light bulb from a table and smashing it on the floor.

The Futurians lectured me severely about this—they said that Lowndes always walked around barefoot, and might have cut himself.

On the way back from Denver, probably at the Mark Twain Hotel in St. Louis—an incredible place—we had picked up bedbugs. We fought them with kerosene in Flit sprayers, and Lowndes recorded our defeats and victories in the Embassy wall newspapers.

Lowndes: "I remember one time I was sick in bed a day or two, lying there feeling very sick, watching a bedbug slowly walking up the wall, and knowing it was eventually going to walk all the way across the ceiling and drop on the bed. That gave me a sort of feeling of Lovecraftian horror. Come to think of it, it was more like Poe—'The Pit and the Pendulum.' "

Michel volunteered to be my guide in New York; he took me for a ride on the El, borrowed a dollar, and said, "Don't tell Donald." He introduced me to Fred Pohl in his apartment in Knickerbocker Village, where we found him typing on a huge impressive machine—I suppose it was only an upright manual typewriter, but it was twice the size of my Royal portable, and looked new. He showed no irritation at being interrupted; he was affable and friendly. Pohl was growing bald in his early twenties, and Michel informed me that it was because he took a shower and washed his hair every morning.

Pohl was free-lancing at this time, having lost his job at Popular. As he explained it later, "I went in to see Harry Steeger in the spring of 1941, determined to get a raise or quit. And he complained that I wasn't coming in early enough; he wanted me to come in earlier or he was going to fire me. And I don't know whether he fired me or I quit, but when I went out of his office I wasn't working there. For about seven months, and then Al Norton sent me a telegram for some reason, I guess he couldn't find my name in the phone book or something—I always meant to ask him why he sent me a telegram—and offered me a job as his assistant. I think I'd been getting twenty dollars a week, and he paid me thirty-five."

I once got a telegram from Norton, too, and I think he just assumed, not unreasonably, that the Futurians didn't have telephones.

Somebody, I have now forgotten who, took me over to the Ravens' Roost, where we found Dick Wilson sitting with Jessica Gould on his lap; she was dark-haired, pretty and plump, and I remember thinking that Wilson must have a lap of iron. I had met him previously at Far Rockaway; he had just come out of the cold ocean and was red, white and blue.

A few months later Wilson and Jessica were married and moved into Knickerbocker Village, across the court from the Pohls.

The Futurian Society as I found it was more like an extended family than like an organization in the usual sense; it had very little formal structure, but it had a tradition, folklore, and a strong sense of us-against-them. Somebody, probably Cyril, had made a plaque with the Futurian coat of arms: it consisted of a large screw, with the legend, *"Omnes qui non Futurianes sunt."* (All who are not Futurians.)

We also had a mock genealogy of the "Conway family," inspired by the Conway Cabal against General Washington during the Revolutionary War: Wollheim, whose creation this was, was Roger Conway, etc. Once or twice these names were used as pseudonyms. The genealogy begins in 1746 with Do-Or-Be-Damned Conway's marriage to Excelsior Prayve-Switchett, who gave birth in 1747 to F. Orlin Conway (hanged in 1773 for horse-stealing). Later descendants include T. O'Conor Sloan, John W. Campbell, and F. Orlin Tremaine. I appear as Ritter Conway, born the year after my mother, Clitoria Conway, went for a ride with a "nice man with a green beard."

In Eugene, Oregon, where my wife and I moved while I was in the middle of this book, a new acquaintance told us about a friend of his who moved from Cleveland to Eugene but went back after six months because he couldn't stand the lack of hostility. Then I realized what it was that seemed different about the Oregonians; I had been away so long that I had forgotten. I remember having a similar reaction to the people I met in California when I lived there for a year in the fifties: they seemed bland, like tapioca. I was used to the Futurians, whose emotional relationships were a heady brew of affection, sympathy, respect, hostility, resentment, malice, and spite.

At the Embassy there was a paradoxical feeling of close attachment and suspicion. The Futurians, at least in my experience, seldom unburdened themselves to each other. Wollheim was locked behind a mask of cold watchfulness; Lowndes concealed his hurts behind a sneer; Michel moved in a cloud of fake charm and bonhommie. Kornbluth was an exception. He enjoyed trading insults, and seldom lost a bout, but when we were alone together he changed completely; he was open, simple, and honest.

By the time I became a Futurian the familiar comedy had begun again. Sykora was inactive and no longer the enemy, although we kept his memory green in song and story. Because there had to be an enemy, a coolness had begun to make itself felt between the two strongest personalities in the Futurian Society, Wollheim and Pohl. Each had his supporters and friends: Wollheim's were Lowndes, Elsie, Michel, Kornbluth and me; Pohl's were his wife Doris, Dick and Jessica Wilson, Rosalind and Harry Dockweiler, Dave Kyle, and Jack Gillespie. Cohen, Burford, and one or two others who came around occasionally, were by this time perceived as hangers-on, not real Futurians.

Old resentments against Pohl contributed to this coolness, but I think the main difference we saw between our group and Pohl's was that we were still essentially bohemians—not regularly employed, poor, and (except for Wollheim) without women. All the members of Pohl's group except Gillespie and Kyle were married, employed, and relatively prosperous.

Curiously enough, the only member of Pohl's faction who dropped in with some regularity at the Embassy was Pohl himself. I'm not sure whether he did this because he enjoyed our company, or because he liked walking into the lions' den.

I remember one evening when we were walking down to Times Square from 103rd Street, five or six of us in a row. I dropped back to tie my shoelace, and when I caught up, embarrassed by calling attention to myself, I had my hands behind my back and was flapping one against the other. Pohl, who was talking to Wollheim, glanced at me and said, "Go flap somewhere else."

On these expeditions, on cool summer nights, we admired the illuminated signs on Broadway, including the one that showed animated cartoons in a grid of light bulbs; then we had coffee at the 42nd Street Cafeteria and walked all the way back. It used up an evening, and cost us only a nickel apiece.

I remember an afternoon when Kornbluth and I, Donald and Elsie and Lowndes were all in the living room; Lowndes was working on an editorial for the next issue of *Future,* and

Cyril, at another typewriter, was setting down his version of the dialogue. I kept that sheet of paper for years, but when I came to write this book I couldn't find it, and have had to reconstruct it from memory.

Lowndes is behind the table, facing the windows, pipe in his mouth; Donald and Elsie sit close together to his left; Donald's arm is around her, and when he tickles or strokes her she utters delighted protests. I am opposite Lowndes, and to my left, in an armchair, Cyril sits with his portable typewriter on his lap. This is what he writes. It is satirically embellished, but not much—it is almost a verbatim transcript.

LOWNDES *(farts):* Excuse me. Got to write the editorial for *Future.* Who shall I write about this time? What about you, Donald?

WOLLHEIM: Sure. Tell them about the time I stuck my finger in the dike and saved Amsterdam from drowning.

ELSIE: Stop it, Donald!

LOWNDES: Well, actually, what I had in mind was more— *(farts)* excuse me.

ELSIE: Stop it, Donald.

WOLLHEIM: Shut up, you. Tell them about the time I shot Bill Hickock in the back.

KNIGHT *(self-consciously):* Why not write an editorial about me?

KORNBLUTH *(laughs heartily):* Yeah, why not?

WOLLHEIM: Tell them about the time I loaned Pierpont Morgan three million dollars and saved the railroads. Tell them about the time I ran off with Jenny Lind.

LOWNDES *(types furiously):* And so, in tribute to Donald A. Wollheim, litterateur extraordinary, savior of science fiction . . . *(farts)* excuse me.

ELSIE: Stop it, Donald!

I remember an impromptu debate with Johnny Michel, who undertook to defend the proposition that a dead dog is not a dog. He let me horse him around from one inconsistency to another for half an hour, then conceded with a grin.

One of Johnny's poses was that of the man of the world; another was that of the bohemian poet. He wore sandals and corduroy jackets with leather elbow patches, and told us about his romantic conquests. His usual attitude toward us was one of tolerant good humor, demonstrating his superior wisdom, but when anything annoyed him, his face contracted in a petulant scowl. His stammer was only a slight hesitation at most times, but when he became nervous or excited he struggled painfully with some fricative or plosive.

His father, a stubble-cheeked little man who wore a beret at work, was the art director at Woolworth's—he produced all their posters and signs by silk-screen, and it was in his shop that Michel ran off covers for fan magazines.

Everything about Michel was small and neat—hands, head, feet. His hands and fingernails, I remember, were always painfully clean; they looked not merely scrubbed but boiled. He kept his room at the Embassy cleaner than anyone else's, and when he roomed with Larry Shaw, later, he insisted on a thorough housecleaning every other day.

He was an ugly drunk. Once in the early forties Pocket Books held an anniversary cocktail party in the penthouse of the RCA Building; Wollheim, who had been invited, gave his tickets to Michel and me. Michel made himself unpleasant to Jan Struther, the author of *Mrs. Miniver,* and to Marion Hargrove; then he tipped over the cake, exposing its plywood base, and we left.

My first contribution to the Futurian wall newspapers was called *The Futurian Embassy Assorted Flug & Chop Suey Drip-*

pings, dated July 28, 1949 [sic—really 1941]. It had a pencil caricature of a libidinous Lowndes under the headline "LOWNDES DEAD!!" Another story concerned Cohen's biting a breakfast-food premium:

> While unsuspectingly tearing into a large bowl of cereal at the Futurian Embassy Saturday, Chester C. Cohen, former diamond merchant, bit into and slightly damaged a so-called "Presidential Coin" maliciously concealed in the stuff.
>
> "My tooth is fractured," Chester alleged. "I will sue. I'll make the fucking bastards pay for this with their last fucking cent, goddamit!" Here Mr Cohen's statement became unprintable.

There was also a report of a formal Futurian meeting, at which Michel was elected director, Wollheim treasurer, Lowndes secretary, Pohl official editor, and Kornbluth member at large.

> Present at the meeting were two factions: Lowndes, Michel, Wollheim, Kornbluth and Chester Cohen for the Center faction, and Pohl, Leslie Perri, Rubinson and Dan Burford for the combined Right and Left.
>
> Two applicants for FSNY membership were proposed at the general meeting: Robert Studley for full membership and Damon Knight for pro tem membership. Both were present at the meeting. Studley was elected; Knight's application was voted down.
>
> At the executive meeting following, however, Knight and stf artist Barbara Hall were proposed and accepted for pro tem membership.

Barbara Hall, a good-looking blond woman, did two scratchboard illustrations for Wollheim's magazines. I don't remember anything about this meeting, and report it as fact only because I wrote the article myself.

In *Futurian War Bulletin,* dated August 9, 1941, Lowndes expressed optimism about the campaign against the bugs: "For over two weeks, continual violations of our frontiers have been made, despite our attempts to establish peaceful relations with these creatures who seek our very life blood. . . . Today our troops administered a defeat to the invader, but that is not enough. The invader must be totally obliterated; no quarter must be given. So long as one of these vermin remain alive, we are in danger, for there can be no treaty or business relations with these blood suckers."

My *Futurian Embassy Fantasy Fiction Flug,* dated August 14, 1941, again had a center-column illustration, this one a penny-arcade photograph of Kornbluth, under the headline "KORNBLATZ TAKES RAP!!"

Cyril Q. Kornbluth, alias Cecil Cornblatz, alias S. D. Gottesbaum, was sentenced today to not more than twenty or less than fifty years in the New York State Penitentiary for the Criminally Insane.

Sneering coldly at judge and jury, the man who left a three-block-wide trail of arson, rape and murder down the middle of Manhattan in a two-week crime spree received his sentence in silence.

Kornbluth, alias Cornblatz, alias Gottesbaum, wore a white silk shirt open at the neck, slacks and riding boots. Thruout the procedings [sic] he showed no other sign of emotion than slowly gnawing the edge of the table-top into splinters.

I found out later that Cyril was worried about his mental stability, but I had no way of knowing that then. I offer this as evidence of the Futurians' instinctive ability to get under each other's skin.

Lowndes told me, "There was a Cabal—Donald, Cyril, John, Chet Cohen and myself. We met once a week. The Cabal was a literary workshop, really. We met at Cyril's place once a week, and each one of us was supposed to bring a manuscript to be read."

I know that the group met at least once at the Embassy, because I was excluded and had to stay out of the living room. And I remember that Cyril called it the Inwood Hills Literary Society, but that may have been a joke. I don't recall Cohen's being a member—maybe he wasn't by the time I got there.

"And as it turned out," Lowndes said, "a fair number of manuscripts that were read at the Cabal were later sold and published. Chet Cohen did provide one story which the Cabal felt, well, might be able to sell, and it was sold, because I accepted it and published it. If either Donald or myself felt a story was good enough to use, we'd accept it on the spot. It was at a Cabal meeting that my story, 'The Leapers,' was read, and the only compliment I remember ever getting from Cyril Kornbluth—he read it, he sort of blinked and shook his head, and said, 'It's *absorbing.*' "

This Futurian pattern of mutual help and criticism was part of a counterculture, opposed to the dominant culture of professional science fiction writers centering around John Campbell. Out of it later came the Milford Conference and the Clarion Workshop, both still viewed with alarm and suspicion by Campbell writers.

The Futurians would have been happy to be part of the

Campbell circle, but they couldn't sell to him;* their motto, in effect, was "If you can't join 'em, beat 'em."

Asimov, the only one of the group who did become a Campbell writer in the early forties, drifted out of our orbit. I never met him until years later, and didn't know he had been a Futurian until the 1956 convention in New York, when he came over to me after the awards ceremonies and told me I had left one name—his—off my list in *In Search of Wonder* of Futurians who had become novelists. Then he kissed me on the ear.

It may be that the Futurians suspected me of unregenerate slovenliness from the first and that I was on probation without knowing it; at any rate, the only time anyone offered to collaborate with me was when Michel, one evening over wine at the Jumble Shop, suggested that we work together on his story, "His Aunt Thiamin." When I timidly reminded him of this the next day, he shook his head and muttered, "I *must* have been drunk."

We played poker for stakes of 15¢ an evening, and because it was hot, we sometimes sat around in our underwear. This must have been the cause of the vice raid that took place in the late summer of 1941.

"There I was, sitting reading *Planet Stories,*" said Lowndes, "and all of a sudden the front window was flung open and somebody came in, pulled out a badge and said, 'Police. Open the front door.'

"I was sort of stunned, and he had to repeat it. So I finally

---

*Perhaps with good reason. Pohl told me that he once took Kornbluth around to see Campbell, and that all through the interview Kornbluth was aggressively rude. Afterward Pohl asked him why, and Kornbluth said, "I wanted to make sure he remembered me."

went and opened the front door, and a line of them sort of filtered in."

I asked, "How many?"

"Do you think I counted them? I'd say four or five. It was very much like *The Trial.* Obviously we were being accused of something, but it was not clear what. Little by little, it began to come clear to me that we were being accused of being homosexuals. I was being asked provocative questions, to which I expressed incomprehension. Finally they looked into the bathroom. The bathroom was plastered with photographs of unretouched female nudes. Michel came in and started to put on a big indignation act, and he was squelched and had the sense to shut up.* They finally decided there was nothing here for them and slithered out, taking some of the most appealing photographs with them. They'd never looked into the closet. If they had, they would have found stacks of Communist literature."

We occasionally drank highballs or cocktails in bars, probably at about 15¢ each—much later, about 1949, they were a quarter in East Side saloons—but I never knew anybody in the Embassy or the later Futurian apartments to buy a bottle, and in fact, when I visited the Blishes in Milford in the mid-fifties and saw that they had a couple of fifths in a kitchen cabinet, I took this as an astonishing sign of affluence.

I remember a Christmas party at Pohl's Knickerbocker Village apartment, where Cohen and I were dropping shot glasses of whisky into glasses of beer in the kitchen. Meanwhile, in the living room, Dockweiler and Jack Gillespie were having a

---

*I heard about this later, and I remember that Michel said he was there at the time of the raid, and that it was difficult to argue with a policeman when you were in your underwear, but never mind.

contest to see who could hold his arm out longest in a Nazi salute. This went on for some time, perhaps as much as half an hour; then Dockweiler motioned with his head to Rosalind and she pushed both their arms down.

Knickerbocker Village was a clean, bright, new housing development; the rooms were clean, bright and new, and so were the tenants. The Pohls and the Wilsons had apartments that faced each other over a courtyard; their "come on over" signal was a dishtowel hung in the kitchen window.

Later, when Dockweiler and Rosalind were married, the group was complete. Fred and Harry were old friends and kindred spirits. Both Rosalind and Jessica admired Doris, who seemed to them a superior person, full of esoteric wisdom. "She was often cruel," Jessica told me, "but I took the cruelty with the occasional confidences and kindnesses she bestowed. I was extremely fond of Frederik—he was witty (except before his morning coffees, at least three) and he was occasionally supportive and always good company. Even in his early twenties he was balding; he reminded me rather of a praying mantis in appearance, though once he began talking that was irrelevant."

This sounds like the ideal recipe for sophisticated young-married living, but it was not quite like that. The Wilsons quarreled, according to Rosalind, and Jessica sometimes broke dishes. Rosalind herself admits that she quarreled constantly with Dockweiler. After about a year Pohl became interested in another woman; then, Jessica says, "Doris was hurt, and she turned to Dick, and then I was hurt."

Moral attitudes in the Futurian Society were curiously mixed. Wollheim was a strict monogamist who vehemently disapproved of premarital sex or cohabitation. He was lenient toward Michel, perhaps because they were old friends and he knew he couldn't change him; even in Michel's case, however, he found other grounds for breaking up a liaison with Judith Merril. Kornbluth, like the rest of us, saw nothing wrong with cohabitation, but he condemned adultery, and he also disapproved of telling dirty jokes in mixed company. This was a cause of friction with Asimov, who was always bawdy whether women were present or not, although his writing was perfectly pure (whereas Kornbluth's tended to be ribald). Cohen and Burford frequented prostitutes; they made Saturday night visits to Harlem, and took me along once or twice; this was considered low behavior by the others.

All the males except Wollheim listened to and repeated dirty jokes, much as we drank and swore, because we considered it daring; but most of us preferred obscenity in invective or wit. Pohl once sat down at the typewriter in my apartment and wrote:

> *Pig-piss and dog shit,*
> *Goat-turds and slime,*
> *Menses of sick whores,*
> *Priced three for a dime:*
> > *These are the pustulent parts of the wight,*
> > *Damon Knight.*

In the fall of 1941 the Futurians held one of their rare formal meetings in the Embassy. I remember it as an election of officers, and so described it in my contribution to *Hell's Cartographers.* Lowndes remembers it the same way, and yet when I began to think about it, it seemed unlikely that it could have been an election: for one thing, Pohl, whom I remember as running against Wollheim, showed up all alone—none of his supporters were there.

I vividly remember the preparations for the meeting. Michel typed up, mounted on colored pasteboard, and tacked to the walls several brief derogatory accounts of Pohl's past actions, in the Futurian Society and in the YCL. I drew a large poster with a skull-face representing Pohl, and the legend, "Uncle Freddie Wants YOU!" I also made a linoleum cut of a skull-face and with it, in dark blue ink, printed several yards of the toilet paper in the bathroom.

Wollheim's explanation of the meeting is this: "Fred had invented the Futurian Federation of the World, which was to be a national Futurian organization, and we had authorized it with the understanding that he was going to do all the work. He was going to put out a fanzine, for which he took subscriptions. And when he got fed up with it, he sent out a postcard poll to all the members of the Futurian Society, to get them to agree to take over these obligations. We hastily called a meeting for the purpose of preventing this, so we wouldn't get loaded with his lousy debts. And that was the meeting at which he was expelled, for actions contrary to everybody else's interest."

It was also, of course, the final rupture between the two factions.

Wollheim once said that what he had found out from the Ivory Tower experience was that the most important thing was to decide who was going to wash the dishes. At the Embassy, I washed them. Lowndes did all the cooking, and it was not bad; his specialty was Futurian chop suey, made with spaghetti, hamburger, and canned cream of mushroom soup: it was best when it had rotted a day or two in the refrigerator.

I hated washing dishes (now I rather like it), and I hated sweeping floors or any kind of housework. Dustballs accumulated under my bed.

One late afternoon, when Johnny was emerging from the

shower, I flicked a dirty rag at him for a joke. He exploded with anger, kicked me in the leg and cursed me in a high, trembling voice. He was apprehensive about germs because of all his osteomyelitis operations, but I had not thought of that.

Earlier in the day I had been invited to have dinner with a pimply fan and his parents, and I now thought it politic to accept. When I got back, the Futurians had met in council, and they gave me an ultimatum: I must either leave or submit to Futurian discipline. I chose to leave, and moved in next day with Chet Cohen, who was living in the Ravens' Roost.

I remember my time at the Embassy as an endless summer; it sprawls so long in my memory that I was astonished when I realized that I could not possibly have lived there longer than five months. Leaving Oregon for New York, and my parents' guardianship for freedom, was a rite of passage for me—I was reborn in the Futurian Embassy. But on looking back I know that I never spent a winter there; almost all my recollections of the Embassy are of heat and sun, whereas what I remember about the Ravens' Roost is the cold and the biting wind from the East River.

It must have been shortly before my falling out with the Futurians that Cyril and I accepted a dinner invitation from two wealthy bachelors who wanted to meet some science fiction writers. It was not a successful occasion. I was struck dumb, as I usually am in strange company, and the dinner passed mainly in silence. I remember that the bachelors—it never occurred to me at the time to wonder if they were homosexuals—had an aged collie who lay on the rug licking his erect penis, and that the soup was served in silver bowls. As we left, Cyril turned and called back (the bachelors were rather deaf), "Frammis on the frammistan, sir!"

Chester Cohen was tidy by nature, but also very lazy, and he didn't mind my slovenly habits. We got on comfortably together in the Roost; the only thing that caused any friction was Chester's preference for sweet butter, which I hated.

Chet's problem was that he was too bright and too talented for the shipping-clerk jobs which were all he was trained for, and not bright or talented enough to do anything else professionally. He had a number of ways of expressing his dissatisfaction with life. One was to say, "I'm *not* happy. I'm not *happy. I'm* not happy," and so on, *ad inf.,* until someone threw a shoe.

I was getting a small allowance from home, and we were both living on it, since Chester was out of work. I remember the elation when we found we could buy a giant can of Campbell's pork and beans at a grocery a few blocks away, for fifteen cents, which was all we had.

At various times we owned and used a cigarette rolling machine. The cigarettes were always too tight or too loose—either they were impermeable to air, or else the tobacco fell out. When we were too broke to buy a pack of Bugler, we rolled cigarettes out of snipes.

Winter had come, and the wind off the East River was so strong that you had to lean at a forty-five-degree angle against it. When the apartment got too cold, we turned on the hot water in the shower, and it rained, just as it had in Wilson's time.

Chester and I were trying to do science fiction illustrations; we sold several collaborations, signed "Conanight." I got work from Doc Lowndes and from Popular Publications, and later from *Weird Tales,* but it was $5 a side—$5 for a single-page drawing, $10 for a double spread—and I couldn't make a living that way, because it took me a couple of days to make a drawing and ink it in, and then I had to rest and recuperate.

Once I asked Lawrence Stevens, who had just brought one

of his incredibly detailed and elegant illustrations to Popular, how long it took him to do one like that. "Oh, a couple of hours," he said.

One winter evening Kornbluth and Mary Byers came to visit us with a tale of woe. Mary had been in town a month or so, staying with Elsie Balter and her roommate in an apartment we called Bitch Haven, but friction had developed, unforgiveable things had been said; Mary needed a place to stay. Chester and I, feeling like Galahads, offered to take her in.

That night, while I slept, Chester and Charlie Colcord cleaned up the apartment and dumped the debris on the roof. Colcord, who was from Maine, told me, "We carried up two boxes of *duht.*"

Kornbluth came over to see Mary once a week. In between, while Chester was at work, I saw a good deal of her. Presently I fell in love with her, and we necked a little.

A month or so later, at a party, someone told me Chester was acting strangely. When I went over to him, he looked at me glassy-eyed and asked, "Are you my mother?" Mary took him out to stay with his uncle and aunt in New Jersey, but he did not improve there, and went into Bellevue, where he had a course of insulin shock.

I took a furnished room by myself for a while; then, after Chester got out of the hospital, we shared a two-room furnished apartment in Chelsea. We called it the Hatch. Later we moved to another in the same neighborhood, and called it Nome (so that when we left a party, we could say, "We're going Nome").

I found out later that Cyril's affair with Mary had caused him trouble at home, since he was under age; he had come to the Futurians for moral support, but what he had got was a massive dose of moral disapproval from Wollheim and Elsie. Lowndes, though downcast by Mary's rejection of him as a suitor, thought Cyril ought to stick with her and marry her, and in the presence of Wollheim and Michel told him so, when he seemed to be wavering, in terms that "in another age would have required a meeting on the field of honor."

Later, Lowndes told me, "Don said that, for the sake of Futurian solidarity, etc., we could not tolerate this affair and that Cyril would have to be expelled from the Futurians if he continued such delinquency. I went along, as I always did with Donald. Then he said that I would have to break with Mary, because that was the soft spot in our front. I agreed to. The next time she called me up at the office, I broke off relations in a particularly cruel manner.

"Looking back, I find the things I most regret in my life are those occasions when I was intentionally cruel or failed to be kind when just a little effort would have been required. But what I did to Mary was deliberate. After that, I don't believe I saw Cyril again until the times of the Hydra Club."

Top, Harry Dockweiler (Dirk Wylie), 1942. *Above left,* Jessica Gould, c. 1941. *Above right,* Doris Baumgardt, 1942.

Top left, Baumgardt and Pohl, c. 1940. *Top right,* Wollheim and Baumgardt, Riis Park, 1939. *Above,* Wilson and Kyle, 1944. *Opposite top left,* Damon Knight, 1939. *Opposite top right,* Gillespie and Pohl, 1944. *Opposite bottom,* first row: Dockweiler, Michel, Asimov, Wollheim, Levantman; second row: Cohen,

Kubilis, Pohl, Wilson; third row: Kornbluth, Gillespie, Rubinson. The photograph of Kornbluth is atypical because he is smiling. The painting in the background is by John Michel. (Photograph courtesy of Richard Wilson and Syracuse University Library)

Top left, Virginia Kidd (photo by Jay Kay Klein). *Above left,* Judith Merril and her daughter, Ann Pohl, 1957 (photo by Ed Emshwiller). *Above right,* the Ivory Tower, 1939 (photo by Jack Robins).

The Futurian Embassy

ASSORTED FLUG & CHOP SUEY DRIPPINGS

Vol 1, No 1   "we don't like the food, either!"   July 28, 1949

LOWNDES DEAD!!

BUCK POHL WELSHES AGAIN! AGREES TO BUY MS FROM KORNBLUTH, FAILS TO KICK IN!

Kornbluth Annoyed But Calm

EMBASSY, July 28 (HtG) - At the Full Meeting Sunday, it is reported, Frederik Pohl, left-wing member, handed back the story which Cyril Kornbluth had prepared to his instructions with the penciled note, "Reasons for Rejecting: (1) Only 4,800 words, (2) Not funny."

This, Cyril maintains, is highly phoney since the story, "An Old Neptunian Custom," was as can be proven the specified length, and since Frederik had already agreed to do a re-write of the story, injecting humor where needed.

FOUR FUTURIANS WHOOP IT UP IN PENNY-ARCADE SPREE

EMBASSY, July 28 (MoL) - Donald A. Wollheim, Cyril Kornbluth, John B. Michel and protemember Damon Knight spent Sunday night wandering from one penny-in-the-slot place to another. Money spent belonged principally to the last two named.

It was observed during the course of the evening (a) that Kornbluth's grip amounts to 0 lb., (b) that Michel is a deadly marksman, and (c) that Wollheim and Kornbluth cannot play arcade-hockey worth a damn.

lowndes

C COHEN CRACKS CHOPPER! COIN CONCEALED IN CORNIES CAUSES CATASTROPHE!!!!!!!

EMBASSY, JULY 28 (MoL) - While unsuspectingly tearing into a large bowl of cereal at the Futurian Embassy Saturday, Chester C. Cohen, former diamond merchant, bit into and slightly damaged a so-called "Presidential Coin" maliciously concealed in the stuff.

"My tooth is fractured," Chester alleged. "I will sue. I'll make the fucking bastards pay for this with their last fucking cent, goddamit!" Here Mr Cohen's statement became unprintable.

However, Mr. John Michel is said to have been seen in possession of the coin in question the next day, and it is further averred that Mr. Michel (cont pg 2)

EMBASSY, July 28 (UR) - It was reported here today that science-fiction's sterling poet, author, agent and all-around heel, Robert W. (Waist line) Lowndes, died quietly sometime this morning of a pulmonary ailment.

Rumors that death was actually caused by alcohol poisoning may be dismissed as base canards, it is alleged.

Present at his bedside during the last hours were John B. Michel, Donald A. Wollheim Damon Knight and an otherwise unidentified goon named Bluto.

Relatives arrived late this afternoon to claim the body, and will transport it in one piece back to Texas for cremation, it was said.

Lowndes was the author of many science-fiction stories articles, poems, and other crap.

When asked for a statement John B. Michel, Lowndes' closest friend, stated: "He was a good man."

At this point several pictures fell from the walls and a black cloud hovered over the room. Poltergeists are suspected.

FULL MEETING OF FSNY HELD; NEW OFFICERS ELECTED

EMBASSY, July 28 (HtG) - At the first full meeting held since last year, the following officers were elected:

(continued pg 2)

The Futurian Embassy

$1 per copy   FANTASY FICTION FLUG $1.50 per year

Vol 1, No 3   "Mit ein meathook dem guna upen"   August 14, 1941

KORNBLATZ TAKES RAP!!

**LOWNDES DENOUNCED AS FRAUD;
FUTURIAN WAR BULLETIN CALLED
UNADULTERATED PROPAGANDA**

EMBASSY, AUG 13 (BON) - In
an interview today Ritter Conway, publisher of FANTASY FIC-
TION FLUG, stated that claims
made in the so-called "Futurian
War Bulletin" may be dismissed
as pure nonsense.

"Neither I nor my colleagues,"
stated Conway, "are worried o-
ver loss of sales caused by
this would-be competitor. However, we feel it our patriotic
duty to make known to the public certain facts concerning
the news sources made use of
by R. W. Lowndes, editor of
the paper.

Kornbluth

"In his first issue Lowndes
described in great detail several widespread troop engagements
which were not mentioned by any of the regular news agencies,
all of which serve FANTASY FICTION FLUG. In one place the "War
Bulletin" says, 'Today the intelligence division laid before us
(sic) the specific basis of the invaders and we advanced, en-
circling these quietly, without attracting undue attention to
our movements. There can be no doubt that the enemy was caught
by surprise for no attempts at adequate defense was made, all
efforts being directed at anarchic flight toward new bases.'

"After some investigation, reporters for FFF traced down the
source of these grandiose reports. Documentary evidence is in
our offices and may be inspected by anyone at any reasonable
time to prove that their only base in fact is a series of attempts on the part of Lowndes to dislodge bed-bugs and other
vermin from his bed, where they are attracted by Lowndes' no-
toriously filthy habits.

"In conclusion I should like to say, and I say it without
fear of successful contradiction, 'YNGVI IS A LOUSE!'"

* * * * * * * * * * * * *

paid adv.   C O N T E S T   paid adv.

With this issue FANTASY FICTION FLUG inaugurates a
new policy of fantastic reporting. One dollar will be paid to
anyone producing written evidence of a fact in this paper.

EMBASSY, AUG 13 (PSD)
Cyril Q. Kornbluth, al-
ias Cecil Cornblatz, al
ias S. D. Gottesbaum,
was sentenced today to
not more than twenty nor
less than fifty years
in the New York State
Penitentiary for the
Criminally Insane.

Sneering coldly at
judge and jury, the man
who left a three-block
wide trail of arson,
rape and murder down the
middle of Manhatten in
a two-week crime spree
received his sentence
in silence.

Kornbluth, alias Corn-
blatz, alias Gottesbaum,
wore a white silk shirt
open at the neck, slacks
and riding boots. Thru-
out the procedings he
showed no other sign of
emotion than slowly
gnawing the edge of the
table-top into splinters.

When approached for a
statement as he was
leaving the courtrocm,
Kornbluth said: "Yrl-
sqb nx sobshuggum illi-
ngoon. Mark my words!"

CHILDREN'S HOSPITAL,
AUG 13 - Mamie Glutz,
3, and Mario Racic, 5,
two children run down
by Cyril Kornblatz last
Monday in his "Ride of
Terror" died early this
morning, making the 16th
and 17th deaths caused
by Kornblatz in a two-
week period.

"THAT'S FIVE CENTS, ISAAC"

Everybody is supposed to remember where he was when he heard about Pearl Harbor, but I don't; I only know that I was in somebody else's apartment with a few other people, and that Danny Burford, who had been listening to the radio, turned around with a funny look on his face and said, "They've bombed Pearl Harbor."

As I talked to the Futurians in preparation for this book, I began to suspect that there are half a dozen distinct kinds of memory. Some people remember the date of practically everything—Fred Pohl is one of these. I have vivid recollections of certain scenes throughout my life (with absolute blanks in between); I can remember how people looked, where they were sitting, how they spoke. I thought everybody's memory was like this, but apparently that is not so; most people remember their own lives only generally and vaguely; very often they have filled in the blank spots with suppositions that turn out to be untrue.*

None of the Futurians were conscientious objectors except James Blish, who burned his draft card (after his army service) in a ceremony organized by Dwight Macdonald, and none tried to evade the draft. Wollheim, Michel, Lowndes, Cohen and I were 4-F; all the other male Futurians went into the service eventually, and so did two of their wives.

In February 1942, Dockweiler and Rosalind Cohen were married, and six months later he volunteered for the army.

"He had told his mother at some point earlier that there were two things in his life he had to do: one of them was that he had to marry me, and the other was that he had to go to war. He was that kind of a romantic.

"I never thought he would go to war, because his eyes were not correctible to twenty-twenty. And of course I had hysterics."

In Columbia, South Carolina, where he was training as an M.P., Dockweiler was slightly injured when he fell off a jeep, but recovered. Just before he was sent to England, he developed a perineal abscess and was hospitalized for a week.

Wollheim, who had been looking for work since *Stirring* and *Cosmic* folded, was interviewed for a job at Ace Magazines a few weeks before his draft examination in 1942. He passed the pre-induction physical, but the doctors at Governors Island found a heart murmur and sent him home. "They gave me the equivalent of a nickel and said, 'Look, tiptoe out of here and

---

*Some of the Futurians were confused even about the date of Pearl Harbor, which is one of the few dates I am sure of—two thought it was in 1942.

don't drop dead on government property.' And I called my father up and said, 'Look, there's something wrong with me, I want you to listen to this heart—it scared the doctors.' "

Wollheim's father showed him his medical record, and it was then that he learned for the first time that he had had polio when he was five.

While Wollheim was at Governors Island, expecting to be inducted, Ace had called him at home and left a message. He went down for another interview and was hired.

"And the next day I went to work as a professional editor, and I've been one ever since. It was the editor of the detectives and sports magazines who was drafted, so I became the editor of *Ten Detective Aces, Twelve Sports Aces,* and two others, and I ended up becoming to all intents and purposes the editor of the Westerns too, because Ruth Brown, the Western editor, was busy doing something else. I was doing six magazines."

A year or so later, Wollheim pointed out with relish, the Futurians had cornered the sports fiction field—"You, and Fred, myself, and Lowndes, we were editing all the sports magazines in existence, with the exception, perhaps, of the Street and Smith magazines."

Shortly after I left the Embassy, Lowndes and Michel moved to an apartment on 27th Street ("The Futurian Fortress") near the Davenport Free Theatre, where they stayed until 1943; then Lowndes took a place on West 11th, and Michel moved to West 4th.

Although his s.f. magazines had perished, Lowndes was by now the editor of all the Columbia pulps except the love magazines, a job he kept until 1960. (In the early fifties his science fiction magazines were revived and continued to the end of the decade.) Lowndes became famous for what Blish later called "making bricks without straw"—with half-a-cent rates long after Pohl's magazines had gone to a cent, he combed the slush-pile, commissioned cover stories from good writers, and kept his magazines, just barely, from sinking into the dead level of pulpdom. His magazines were an open market for new writers, and many were first published there.

In 1942, after two years of marriage, Fred and Doris Pohl had separated when the lease on their apartment ran out—not for that reason, but it seemed like a good time to do it. Pohl was working as one of Alden Norton's assistant editors, and living in a hotel.

Pohl said about his breakup with Doris: "I think that that split was very close to one hundred percent my fault. I think that if I had been a little more mature and a little smarter and a little better informed about the world, I would have stayed married to her indefinitely. She was a pretty good person, and the reasons why we separated were not real, they were just head stuff; the world was not working out the way I wanted it to, and I was trying to find some way of making it better, by finding somebody else to be married to. Which doesn't really work very well."

In 1942, recently married to Gertrude Blugerman, Isaac Asimov was working as a chemist at the Naval Air Experimental Station in Philadelphia, where Robert A. Heinlein and L. Sprague de Camp also worked as engineers.

"Gertrude would make lunch for me," Asimov recalls, "nice lunches—I remember tongue sandwiches were my delight in those days—and I liked to sit in the chemistry lab and eat at my leisure and read. But Heinlein would not have it. He wanted me to come with the rest to the cafeteria, which was half a mile across the swamp. And it was one of the most hot, muggy summers, and there was no shade, and you walked through that sun there and into the cafeteria, which was huge and noisy, and the food was mediocre, and then when you finished you'd walk back. And it was just the most miserable part of the day for me.

"For one thing, in the old days particularly, I didn't very much enjoy eating with others because there seemed to be all kinds of comments about how quickly I ate. Now I used to eat when I was in the candy store, and it's no use telling me I'm not in the candy store anymore, it's a lifelong habit which I can't break. The point was, you were fed, and since there were others waiting their turn you had to eat fast, and get out and work in the store so someone else could come in. And to this day I don't talk while I eat; I just get on with the job. In fact, when mine is d⌐layed, I always tell everybody, 'Don't worry, no matter how late it comes, I'll be finished first.'

"Once in the cafeteria, there were two halves of a hard-boiled egg in my salad, so I forked up one half and put it in my mouth. I didn't just *put* it in my mouth, but the fork went so fast that you didn't see it disappear. And Leslyn Heinlein said, 'That's terrible, Isaac—you make me want to throw up.' I didn't know to what she was referring. I didn't recall doing anything. So I said to her, 'I'm sorry, Leslyn'—you know, just a general apology, not knowing what I had done. And then I forked up the other half, and she said, 'You've done it *again!*' "

Heinlein objected to Asimov's complaints about the cafeteria food. "He was a gung-ho patriot, and the cafeteria was serving food to war workers, and it was Doing a Good Job. And if you complained about the food, you were sort of a slacker. And believe me, the food was complainable, if you know what I mean. And he finally said to me, 'Look, Isaac, from now on, any time anyone complains about the food, they have to contribute five cents to a kitty, and when it piles up we'll buy a War Bond.' And nobody else complained about the food. So it became then a game, if I could think of some way of complaining about the food which I could maintain was an ordinary comment, so I didn't have to pay five cents. And I got Heinlein to agree that if I ever succeeded, he'd drop the whole thing. But he was the judge, too—no matter what I said, he would claim it was a complaint, and I'd lose five cents. Once, eating their goddamn fish and trying to cut through the skin, I said, in a sort of ordinary tone of voice, 'Is there such a thing as *tough fish?*' And Heinlein said, 'That's five cents, Isaac.'

"Finally, though, I beat him. Some stranger joined the group, and he hadn't taken more than two mouthfuls when he put down his fork and said, 'Gee, this is horrible.' And I jumped up instantly and said, 'I disagree with every word this man has said, but *I will defend with my life his right to say it!*' "

By the end of 1942 the Futurians had written and published a hundred and twenty-nine science fiction stories, nearly all in Futurian magazines. Most of these were collaborations, and nearly all were published under pseudonyms. By the end of 1943 the Futurians had lost all their s.f. magazines; but at their zenith they had controlled more than half the magazines in the field.

By 1943 I had succeeded in selling a few stories and illustrations to Popular Publications; when one of their editors was drafted, Fred Pohl recommended me for the job (and lent me a white shirt to apply in). I was hired at $25 a week. I worked a month or two for Alden Norton; then an assistant editor was needed in Mike Tilden's department and I was transferred there, perhaps partly because the publisher, Harry Steeger, had complained that I was too visible eating my lunch in Norton's bullpen, where my desk faced an open door at the end of the hall.

Steeger was a slender, elegant gray man—gray eyes, gray

hair, gray suit. Another thing he didn't like about me was that we often met in the elevator in the morning, both of us fifteen minutes late.

He must have had some good qualities, because Popular was a happy place to work. Everybody there was likeable and easy to get along with, with two exceptions, both women who had been with the company from the beginning. I understood them better years later when I read James Watson's description of "Rosie" in *The Double Helix*.

Popular's forty pulp magazines were distributed among five departments, each with an editor and several assistants. The head of a department bought stories and scheduled them; after that the assistant editor did all the rest—copyediting, proofreading, filling out forms to be sent to the printer, etc. The assistant was also expected to write for each story a blurb and seven or eight titles, from which his boss would pick one—or perhaps not, in which case he would have to think of seven or eight more. (Often he had to rewrite the blurb, too.) Many of the titles were puns, and after a while I began to see that as a game, and used to make up lists of possible titles in the subway— *We Who Are About to Fry, Where There's a Kill There's a Way,* etc. I liked the crime titles best, because they could be funny. The sports titles and blurbs were the hardest; the technical vocabulary of golf, for instance, is very limited—par, birdie, and so on—; these words had to be combined and recombined constantly in new ways.

After about a year at Popular I couldn't stand the Westerns any more, and I quit. After that I fooled around at home for a while trying to paint. I produced one good canvas, "The Hollow Men"; the rest were daubs. I attempted a portrait of Jim Blish, and he came over for sittings once a week, but the portrait made him look like a Japanese admiral, and I gave it up.

Fred Pohl told me a terrible story. "It was March 1943, and Cyril had been off in Connecticut, where he signed up with a special Army program as a machinist. That sort of stuff interested him a lot; he collected music boxes for a while, and he liked to take them apart and put them together again—fairly delicate little things. And he had friends who did glass engraving with a revolving wheel, and he liked to play with that. I used to have a thing called the 'Pohl Bowl,' which was a signed work by Cyril, but somebody stepped on it. I never saw him swim, I never saw him throw a ball, but he was well enough coordinated to do anything he really wanted to do.

"But anyway, when he was about to go in, he came to New York to say good-bye to everybody. I was living in the Hotel Webster on West 45th Street. He came up to the hotel and we went into some of the bars along Sixth Avenue, and ate the free lunch and had a few drinks, and went to another bar and had a few more drinks, and got very drunk. .

"And next morning I woke up with the worst hangover I have ever had in my whole life—oh, God—and Cyril was in bed with me. And the room was covered with what few bits of our clothing we had taken off, a shirt here and a shoe there, and about half of it was soaked with blood. And Cyril woke up, very pale, and we looked at each other, and I went into the bathroom and turned on the shower and stood under the hot water for about an hour, trying to wake up and put the world back together. When I got out Cyril was dressed, and he said, 'Well, I think I'd better go, Fred. So long, have a nice war.' And I gathered up the bloodiest things and put them in the hamper or something so the chambermaid wouldn't faint, and went off to work at Popular, feeling very fragile. I'd been there about fifteen minutes when the phone rang, and it was Johnny Michel, saying, 'Fred. We will never forgive you for last night.'

"And then gradually it began to come back. And I remembered that we'd been talking about the Futurians, and we'd been talking about Johnny, and maybe you, I don't remember —Lowndes in particular, and Cyril was pissed at Lowndes; and I said, 'What are you mad at Lowndes for?'

"He said, 'I hate him.'

"And we had a few more drinks, and he said, 'I know what we ought to do, we ought to kill Lowndes.'

"And I said, *'Fine.* Let's kill Lowndes. Let's have a drink first.' So we went up to my room with a bottle and we had a couple of drinks, and Cyril said, 'Listen. I really mean it, I want to go kill Lowndes.' and I said, 'Sure, Cyril. Here's the bottle. Pour another drink.'

"He said, 'You're going to chicken out, aren't you.'

"I said, 'No, I'm not going to chicken out.'

" 'Will you swear an oath in blood?'

"So I said, *'Right,* I'll swear an oath in blood,' and I went in the bathroom and got a safety razor blade, and nicked my thumb. Cyril drank a drop of my blood, and took the blade— *whow!* ripped a big slice out of his hand, and wrapped it up with something: that was where all the blood came from.

"And then we went down to kill Lowndes. We went out and got on a Fifth Avenue bus down to 28th Street. I remember trying to pick up a girl on the bus, and I really shudder at how I must have seemed to her—she was a pretty, young, inoffensive girl, sort of crouched into a corner at the top of the Fifth Avenue bus.

"And I remember getting as far as the building, and Cyril rattling the gate, and both of us yelling up to Lowndes, 'Come on down so we can kill you.' And that's all I remember.

"I remember what the bars were, and I remember we got thrown out of a couple of them, one on Sixth Avenue and one on 42nd Street, the old bar that used to be next to the Forty-second Street Cafeteria, I think it was called the Forty-second Street Bar. We got thrown out of that one because we ate up all their free lunch: they took a dim view of that. Then we went to some other bar, presumably down near where the Futurians were living, and the bartender wouldn't serve us a drink; and Cyril said, 'Ah, come on now, you're a fine Irishman, you'll serve an Irishman a drink, won't you?' And I tried wheedling the Irish fellow too, but he wasn't deceived for a second, he knew we weren't Irish. And we tried a few shure and begorrahs on him, and went out.

"I think Lowndes wasn't there. I think maybe Johnny was there by himself, scared shitless."

Some time before this Pohl had met a girl from Florida named Dorothy Les Tina. "We had more or less made up our minds to get married," he said, "early in '43, when she went into the WACs and I went into the Army, and we saw each other very rarely. And I was shipped to Italy; some months later she was shipped to Germany. And I wanted to see her. Unfortunately she was in the European Theater of Operations, and I was in the Mediterranean Theater. I could travel around anywhere in the Mediterranean, and she could travel anywhere in Europe, but we couldn't cross the border without some special permission. The only way I could get permission was by marrying her. So I explained that and said, 'Do you want to get married?' And she wrote back and said, 'Why not?' So we got married in Paris, by order of the Commanding General, Mediterranean Theater of Operations, U.S. Army. Which was a little sticky, because she was a first lieutenant, and I thought I was a corporal—actually I was a sergeant; I was promoted just before I left, but I didn't know that. So in the caste system of the U.S. Army, it was difficult for us to arrange our honeymoon. Wasn't hard to find a place to stay, it was hard to find a place to eat. Because we couldn't just go into a restaurant in Paris; they didn't have any food. The war was still on, so everything was rationed, you couldn't buy anything without ration books. Service people were supposed to eat in American messhalls. And there wasn't any messhall for both of us.

"We finally wound up eating in a little private dining room in a generals' mess near the Etoile, what is now called the Place Charles de Gaulle. As a result of which we ate better than either of us had in some time. That was in August of '45. In November I was sent back: the war ended shortly after we were married. I spent a couple more months waiting for shipping. I had enough points to be discharged; I had all sorts of battle stars and things, because they handed them out like popcorn in the Air Force, and each one of them was worth a certain number of points, but there wasn't enough shipping. So I hung around there doing nothing much until November, and then I was sent back, and discharged on my birthday in 1945.

"And Tina was sent back along about February or March, and we rented an apartment in Greenwich Village, which cost a hundred seventy-five dollars rent, and I was being paid fifty dollars a week with taxes deducted from that. I worked for an advertising agency called Thwing and Altman. They had mostly book accounts: the Dollar Book Club, Junior Literary Guild, William H. Wise, Merriam-Webster Dictionary, stuff like that. And the reason I was there was, while I was in the Air Force in Italy, I got homesick for New York, because I had a lot of time on my hands. And I thought I'd write a novel about the advertising business. So I wrote it: dreadful novel. And somehow I came to the conclusion that there might have been something wrong about it, since I didn't know anything about the advertising business, so when I got to be a civilian, I bought a Sunday *Times* and looked up the ads for advertising agency personnel, and I answered three ads and one of them hired me as a copywriter.

"So in a four-Friday month I was receiving something like eight dollars less than my rent, and I had to scrounge around and make a little extra money."

Pohl wrote for the pulps awhile, then got another job at *Popular Science.*

"I was there three years or so as assistant circulation manager and book editor and some other title, I've forgotten what. I was in charge of the book fulfillment department [in the industry, this odd phrase just means the department where book orders are filled], which was one Seventh Day Adventist and twenty-five silly girls. The reason they had the Seventh Day Adventist was that they couldn't trust anybody else with the twenty-five silly girls. He was a nice guy, except that in the winter he'd have to leave early so as to be home by sundown. And I stayed there until '48 sometime, when I quit to run the [Dirk Wylie] agency full time."

Mildred Virginia Kidd was born in 1921, in Philadelphia, the third living child of Charles and Zetta Daisy Whorley Kidd. Six months later her father moved the family to Baltimore, where he opened a successful printing business.

When Kidd was two, she contracted polio. "I was totally paralyzed, rolled up into a tight ball; four doctors tried to straighten me out but were unable to unlock me from the tight foetal position." She was paralyzed a long time, bedridden for years. "My mother and father massaged my right leg interminably; the smell of cocoa butter still turns my stomach." Her left arm and leg recovered completely, but she had to wear a brace on the right leg until she was six.

"I have a vivid recollection of standing across the street from our house, taking a step and feeling the brace disintegrate and fall around my foot. I picked up the brace and walked home carrying it, and never wore it again. The feeling, 'I'm walking, I can walk, I'm walking by myself,' was almost akin to 'I'm flying'—equally as triumphant."

In high school she was active and popular, a sort of teacher's pet, without being disliked by her peers. "The same was not true at home. My older brother and sister disliked me heartily, and with good reason. Because I was crippled, my father and mother appeared to feel that I could do no wrong—whatever I did my brother and sister got blamed for, even if I confessed."

When she was nine she read a science fiction magazine belonging to her brother, and became a convert. Two years later she began writing letters to the magazines, and through the letter columns acquired a list of correspondents that at one time reached a total of fifty-two. One of them was Robert W. Lowndes. At sixteen, she was engaged to him by correspondence.

"And my mother handled it the best way possible—she said, 'Oh, that's very interesting,' and began to laugh. I went up to my room and thought about this for a while, and then wrote him a very solemn letter saying I had changed my mind."

In the choir at the Unitarian Church she met a handsome baritone, Jack Emden. She was living then with her married sister in Baltimore. "I worked at a number of bars in East Baltimore, unbeknownst to her, using the name and social security number of a friend; it was a wild and sexually very exploratory summer. I was living a number of lives superimposed on one another, with language school in the daytime, working in the bars at night, singing in the choir on Sunday, and attending dancing lessons to strengthen my leg.

"Jack and I were lovers for two years, and might have broken up then, except that he decided to enlist just after Pearl Harbor, and with his exaggerated sense of responsibility, Jewish-son duty, he decided we should be married."

She "camp-followed" him around the country until he was shipped overseas; then, pregnant, she came to New York, where the first thing she did was to buy a bunch of science fiction magazines.

"Hadn't you been reading them?" I asked her.

"No, not for the last couple of years; while I was a young bride I was interested in nothing but my husband and what I was doing in various cities, where I had an interesting job in each city. And I don't remember whether it was a science fiction magazine or whether in sheer desperation I had picked up a Western magazine—it might have been a Western—and saw Bob Lowndes's name on the masthead. So I went into one of those little kiosks on the street that used to work—now none of them do—and I phoned him, and it was very funny, because the minute I heard his voice, I said, 'You have a *mustache.*' And he did.

"I had been on my way to New York City from the time I was in seventh grade, and I got there by a very roundabout route, via Tucson, Miami, and Greenville. I was in a hospital in Greenville for two or three days when I was two or three months pregnant, and the hospital was so crowded, they put me in the maternity ward, although there was no question of my delivering at that point, I was just in danger of a miscarriage; and I was right next door to a room where they were delivering babies South Carolina style. And what I heard convinced me that I wanted to go to New York and have that Yankee baby.

"There was a pitiful scene in the parlor of the boardinghouse I was living in, with all these Southern people who had grown very fond of me during the months I was living there, and I of them, saying, 'Don't go and let that little *ba*yabee be a *Ya*yankee!' But I took off at seven months pregnant for New York City, and having experienced a South Carolina spring, I arrived in April or May, and the tree in the back yard of the apartment I rented immediately came into leaf for me, and I had a New York spring.

"I had been on my way to New York for ever so many years. Marrying Jack and going around the country with him was a side issue, something that came in the way, on the way, but as soon as he went overseas I decided to go from South Carolina to New York—it was the only place I could possibly have gone."

Josephine Judith Grossman (later Judith Merril) was born in Manhattan in 1923, the daughter of Samuel S. and Ethel Hurwitch Grossman. Samuel Grossman, usually called Schlomo (for Solomon, his middle name), was the son of a well-known Philadelphia rabbi. Ethel Hurwitch, an immigrant from Russia at the age of five, had grown up in Boston.

"My father was a writer in the Jewish education field," Merril told me, "drama critic for *The Vorwärts,* things like that—my mother was an early suffragette, one of the founding members of Hadassah. My mother and father met when they were working for the then-infant Bureau of Jewish Education in New York, in the great golden days of the idealist Zionist movement, into which I was born. My father had encephalitis in the epidemic that followed the flu epidemic in the years after World War I, which meant that he was acutely ill in the hospital at the same time that I was born, and apparently suffered severe aftereffects in terms of a loss not of writing talent but quickness—and certainly confidence—a psychiatric rather than an intellectual loss. And having been up to that point sort of the fair-haired boy of American Jewish writing, he quickly slid out of that position, and within a few years after my birth we had wound up going to live with relatives, since my father was not earning any money. This was in Boston; we were living with my mother's father, and her sister. I don't remember when we moved there, I must have been four or five.

"When I was six, he committed suicide at a very dramatic moment. He had been for three months daily submitting a fifteen-minute news broadcast in rhymed verse to a radio station—they wanted a three-month trial period before deciding that he could actually do it day by day—he had a particular talent for doggerel. And he went to the building that day to get a definite yes or no, and they were on the sixteenth floor. And he couldn't face the possible rejection, apparently, and got out on the fifteenth floor and jumped out the window. And that left a difficult situation all around.

"So my mother and I were poor relations here and there for a while. She took a dietetics course and we began living in various institutions where she worked—orphan asylums and things like that—a summer camp where she was dietitian was near Milford. When I was thirteen she got a job in a settlement house in the Bronx, which is what took us to New York, where I discovered the YPSLs.* I was born a Zionist, in those golden days of socialist Zionism, and until I was in my early teens at least, knew that my future was in a kibbutz: I was preparing for it, and studied Hebrew until I was about fifteen, by which time I had progressed from social Zionism to socialism to the

---

*Pronounced "Yipsls": members of the (Trotskyist) Young People's Socialist League, or YPSL.

YPSLs, and no longer knew that my future was in a kibbutz.

"When I was about fifteen, it dawned on me that my mother meant for me to be a writer, and I stopped writing completely, and I didn't start again until after I had a baby and I was in San Francisco and my mother was in New York."

In 1940 she married a YPSL friend and went to live with him in Philadelphia. Her husband was a science fiction reader; she was not, until illness kept her in bed for a few days. "It was the middle of winter," she told me, "and I had the grippe, and I had a toothache. And I couldn't do anything about the toothache because I couldn't get out of bed—I wasn't desperately sick at that point, but I wasn't well enough to go find a dentist. I had read everything in the house that I considered readable, so I finally opened a couple of his magazines, and that was the beginning of the end. The magazines I happened to open had an installment of *The Stolen Dormouse,* by L. Sprague de Camp, and an installment of Heinlein's *Methuselah's Children,* and I don't remember what else, but that was enough. As soon as I was well, ignoring the dentist, I went down to the secondhand magazine store and got some more."

In 1941 they moved to New York, where their daughter Merril was born the following year. Judy took her daughter's name as a pseudonym, later adopted it legally. When her husband went into the navy in 1945, Judy followed him first to Chicago and then to San Francisco. Her husband was shipped out to the submarine base at Pearl Harbor; Judy returned to New York with her child and took an apartment in Greenwich Village. A friend of hers from Philadelphia, who knew she was interested in science fiction and in writing, introduced her to John Michel. Presently she began an affair with him, with her husband's knowledge; they had made an agreement about temporary sexual freedom while he was overseas.

She told me, "I can remember Johnny stopping two or

three steps out on the street—we were going toward his apartment, and Johnny stopped to declaim on how exceedingly old he felt, and this quite dismayed me because he was twenty-seven. I thought, My God, will I feel that way when I reach that age?

"Another memory is going into the subway with Johnny and having a terrific battle because I insisted on paying my own fare. It was the first time I went anywhere with him—he got very upset about it—assured me that I would never do that again if I went anywhere with him."

This was an oddity in a dedicated Marxist and Russophile, but Michel had some peculiarly retrograde ideas about women. At this time, in the early forties, he had abandoned science fiction as unprofitable and was making a rather thin living by writing aviation articles.

Merril said, "The way I wrote and sold my first story—this was a detective story for *Crack Detective*—Johnny had been persuading me that I should try to write a story, and I had tried this, and then he brought Bob [Lowndes] up to read it. And Bob said, 'If you do some revision, I can buy this story.'

"And he sat down and completely broke down the story for me. What it needed was complete breakdown and reassembly, and he did this with such patience and skill that, simply following instructions, I was able to rewrite it so that he could and did buy it. Before I showed it to him again, after the first rewrite, Johnny came in and went through it with a much sharper scalpel—and I think I learned more from that one session with Johnny than I learned for years afterwards until I had a couple of similar sessions about poetry with [Theodore] Sturgeon."

Early in their relationship, Michel took Merril out to Forest Hills to meet the Wollheims, now married and living in a fashionable apartment with a sunken living room. Merril told me, "It was more like being taken home to his family than anything to do with the Futurians; I think I was supposed to get Donald and Elsie's approval. I remember it was quite a gruesome experience. The only interesting thing about the visit was Elsie showing me jewelry weights, and explaining some of the things she did in her father's shop.

"I still feel that Johnny was potentially one of the most interesting and talented people there, and there was some real lack of confidence, or self-direction or something, that just kept him from going anywhere, and made him do things like obeying Donald."

I asked her what she thought of the Futurians as a group, and mentioned that in *Hell's Cartographers* I had called them "a gallery of grotesques."

"The Futurians were a very motley crew," she said, and Virginia Kidd, who was sitting beside her in my living room, put in, "Almost everybody was callow, one way or another."

"Callow, or extremely unattractive, or both," said Merril. "I felt I belonged very much in such a group, and I think this was characteristic of everyone there, that each of us regarded ourselves as grotesque, and felt comfortable in a gathering of grotesques."

Kidd said reminiscently, "At one point I was working with Johnny on an article—I was doing the typing, he was doing the note-taking—something to do with aviation. And I believe we were pacing along the corridors of the library, busily talking about the article, when he stopped and said, 'Virginia, you realize I can't go to bed with you, because you're politically unconscious.' Nothing was farther from my mind."

"MY GOD, EARS!"

James Blish was born in 1921, in East Orange, New Jersey, the only child of Asa and Dorothea Schneewind Blish. He was "some fractional part" Jewish on his mother's side; his maternal grandfather, Benjamin von Schneewind, was a candy manufacturer who packaged two large boxes of chocolates, very popular in the Midwest at one time, named the Dorothea and Babette Selections after his two daughters.

Asa Blish came from a New England family; the name is a variant of Bliss. He was a publicist in the thirties for Bernarr Macfadden and for Arnold Gingrich of *Esquire*. He and his wife were divorced when James was six.

Dorothea Blish moved to Chicago with her son, and James went to high school there. Dorothea was a talented pianist and piano teacher; she had perfect pitch. She started Jim's musical training early, and at various times he learned to play piano, trumpet, glockenspiel, and French horn. Some time during the late thirties, Blish and his mother moved back to New Jersey; he attended Rutgers and then Columbia.

He went from college into the army (although he burned his draft card later); but did not take well to military discipline; he was always in trouble over unshined shoes, or pajamas showing under his trousers at reveille. At Fort Dix, he did not let the army interfere with his writing: he set up a card table in the canteen, lined up several containers of beer around the edges, with his typewriter in the middle, and wrote for three or four hours every night, while the other draftees were playing pool or listening to the jukebox. The end of his military career came when he refused an order to clean the grease trap under the kitchen sink. Since it was wartime, he could have been court-martialed, but his father pulled strings in Washington and got him discharged.

Blish had been present at Futurian meetings in 1938 and 1939 but had been out of touch since then. When he left the army, the Futurians gave him a dinner party at the Dragon Inn in the Village; I met him there for the first time. In December 1944 Lowndes introduced him to Virginia, "not knowing that I was introducing Tristan to Isolde."

After that, Lowndes said, "Donald, John and I went out to call on him and try to propagandize him into joining the new a.p.a. [amateur press association] which was first 'Gothic,' then 'Modern,' and finally wound up as 'Vanguard.' We were pissed off at the situation in FAPA, and I said to Don, 'Why not start a new a.p.a., and this time keep control of it?' We had tried to introduce amendments to the constitution, one of which would have made racial slurs grounds for immediate expulsion. Anyway, the amendments did not pass, and we felt that FAPA was hopelessly reactionary."

Lowndes and Blish took an apartment together on West 11th Street; they called it "Blowndsh."

"One night," said Lowndes, "rather late—we had finished all the beer—there came a knock on the door, and in came someone from Brooklyn Heights. We listened to music awhile, and Jim said, 'Would you like a cup of coffee?' Well, of course he would, so Jim went out to prepare three cups of coffee. Jim sipped his cup first and said, 'It's not very good.' I sipped mine and said, 'It's absolutely vile.' The guest sipped his and just spat it all over the floor.

"I said, 'Jim, what did you make this coffee with?'

" 'Well,' says Jim, 'there was a pan of water on the stove.'

"I said, 'Oh. That was not water, that was Epsom salts.' I had an infected finger, and I'd been soaking my bandaged finger in that for several days."

Lowndes had a large black cat, Blackout, given to him by Marie Antoinette Park, the love pulp editor at Columbia, to whom he was engaged at the time. Blackout's sex was uncertain.

Kidd told me, "Lowndes used to forget to buy cat food for Blackout, so he'd go down to the deli to get him something to eat—usually salami—and Blackout would get up in my lap and put his paws on my shoulders and exhale garlic in my face.

"One time Jim brought home a white kitten he'd picked up from a bakery or somewhere. Blackout had never seen another cat before. He walked up to it, and this little ball of fluff arched its back and hissed at him. Blackout went straight up to the top of the bookcase, from there to the record cabinet, and from there to a taller cabinet, and stayed there for three days, vomiting frequently."

The white cat was Curfew, also referred to hopefully as Formed Stool Conway.

Lowndes also introduced Merril and Kidd, thinking that they might like to know each other since they were both "war widows" with small children.

Kidd told me, "I went from where I was living on East 46th Street to see Judy on Greenwich Street, in the apartment that had the floors and walls that slanted. I went just for the afternoon, and stayed there three or four days. And we slept the baby in a laundry basket, and became fast friends."

Through Lowndes, the two women gradually met the rest of the group. Since they were both gregarious and lonely, they fell into the habit of entertaining and feeding Futurians.

"I couldn't endure Chester at first," Merril told me. "I don't mind saying this because it's irrational—not like some other people where there were reasons for it. I think it was because you always brought him with you—this was at the very beginning; when I got to know him it was different. But when I first met Chester, I would invite you, and the two of you would show up. And Chester never said anything. Chester came and sat in the corner, on the floor; but there was no conceivable way to invite you without acquiring you and Chester."

Kidd said, "This endeared him to me, because he was so shy."

"Well, it didn't endear him to me—I resented feeding someone I couldn't communicate with. But as I very gradually got to know Chester, and he went from muttering a word to muttering a sentence, he eventually became very entertaining and I became quite fond of him. I met Jim later—either he wasn't around, or I didn't intersect with him."

"He was still living at home in New Jersey then," Kidd said.

"When he moved in with Bob is when I met Jim, I think, or shortly before that."

Kidd told her, "It was Easter, 1945. I remember it very

well, because you threw your arms open, and he threw his arms open and you advanced toward each other and put your arms around each other, and I was *furious.*"

"Jim and I?"

"Yes. It was a gag."

"Must have been," said Merril.

Merril, who was a Trotskyist, and Blish, who described himself as a "book fascist," meaning that he agreed with the theory of fascism, not with its practice, antagonized each other almost on sight.

Merril said, "I thought he was very, very snotty and affected, and I frequently suspected his authoritative information, but I rarely was inclined to go look it up. I remember, probably one-sidedly, a series of sort of weekly discussion things on Greenwich Street, where Jim and I would get into the same political argument each week, and I would beat him to the floor—this is how I remember it—and at the end of it he would say, 'You're right,' and then he would come back the next week and start the same argument all over again, with some one new piece of information. As I say, this is probably a *very* one-sided memory."

Not long afterward Kidd and Merril took adjoining apartments on Washington Street in the Village, and knocked down a wall between two closets to make a passageway. They called the double apartment Parallax; here they took turns entertaining the group on Thursday evenings.

Kidd said, "You know, we figured up to the penny how much we had spent, and that was divided by how many people were there, and the attendees paid thirty-three cents apiece, or forty-eight cents, whatever it came out to, and somebody was expected to wash the dishes. And when it came to be Damon Knight's turn, he stopped being a perfectly healthy young man; in the space of five minutes his tie came askew, and his collar was hanging limp and open, and he had a flush in his cheeks, and his hair got all awry and rumpled—he had to go home, 'cause he was *sick*."

We talked about the fact that the Futurians didn't seem to know any other women. "That's why they were always over at our place," Merril said with a smile. "What strikes me as odd is that a few years later when all these people did know women, I thought it was very disagreeable."

Kidd put in, "I remember those dinners—that period—as one of the happiest periods of my life."

Michel at this time was sharing a Village apartment with Larry Shaw, who had recently moved to New York from Schenectady.

Shaw said, "That came about mainly because Michel had quit a job—he was working for Street and Smith on *Air Trails,* and they put John Campbell in as editor and made it *Air Trails and Space Frontiers,* and Michel hated Campbell, so he quit, and not having any fixed income, decided to take a roommate.

"I probably met Judy through Michel. He always went over to her place. I didn't know what was happening at the time, I only knew he was seeing some woman. Then one day when I was working at *Hat Life* Judy called me up and asked me if I could have lunch with her, so we went to a Chinese restaurant on 23rd Street, and Judy told me. She just felt that I ought to know, for some reason.

"Rooming with Michel did a lot for me in a strange way, because it was one of those periods when he was having those painful abscesses; he was in great pain a lot of the time, and I had to take care of him. I think doing that helped me grow up a good deal. He was pretty much bedridden: he could get up and walk around some, but he had to keep packing the abscesses with Kotex. And he couldn't eat much. I remember one time I went out and just got him a head of lettuce, because that was all he could·eat.

"He was certainly under the influence of Wollheim in a great many ways, but both of them joked about the Communist Party, and the party lines. I remember one small incident when Senator Bilbo was ramping and raving a lot, and a war veteran who was on crutches organized a movement to picket Bilbo. I had quit my job at *Hat Life,* and I wanted to go down to Washington and join the pickets. And Johnny was quite horrified; he said, 'Larry, we talk about things like that, we don't *do* them.'

"Johnny and I and the Wollheims went out to dinner in the Village frequently. Occasionally there would be somebody else along, and Johnny would always make an effort to make sure I was included in the conversation.

"Wollheim was very careful with Johnny, very solicitous. Johnny had the stammer, which got quite bad sometimes. When it got bad, Donald would divert people's attention.

"In many ways, in spite of being a radical politically, Wollheim was one of the most conservative men I've ever known—always being sure he had a job, and presented a good image to the public—warning me against doing anything radical, or having friends who appeared too radical. He disapproved somewhat, if not of you, Damon, at least of the way you were living, and he definitely disapproved of Chester. Chester was just beyond the pale: drank too much, frivolous in his attitudes, didn't take anything seriously. When Donald found out somehow that I had slept with Virginia a couple of times, he gave me a lecture about 'drinking from a dirty cup.' "

Shaw says he was a member of a group called the Arisians (named after the all-knowing aliens in E. E. Smith's "Lensman" series) which Wollheim had started early in 1945*—they were science fiction fans, mostly young, who met at Wollheim's apartment once a month. Their club organ was a magazine called *La Vie Arisienne,* a joke that went over the heads of the young members.

One of the Arisians was Joe Kennedy, now the award-winning poet X.J. Kennedy; another was Russell Wilsey, whom Wollheim remembers as "a really brilliant, erratic type who had some elements of Kornbluth and some of Michel, and who became a good friend and protégé of ours—but eventually made a rather dreadful marriage, went into a morbid tailspin (reminiscent of Cyril and Johnny in some ways), and died of an overdose of sleeping pills in his early twenties." Wollheim hoped the Arisians would form the nucleus of a new Futurian group, but it did not, and the club disbanded after about a year.

Neither Kidd nor Merril remembers seeing much of the Wollheims during this period. Some tension was already growing between Wollheim on one hand, Merril and Blish on the other.

Kidd said, "I have a vivid memory of Donald and Elsie arriving right at dinner time, having been invited to one of our alternate Thursday night dinners, with the smell of garlic on their breath, very strong, and I was sure that they had stopped at a restaurant first and eaten—and they had. And, you know,

---

*Wollheim does not recall that Shaw was ever a member. Another oddity is that Wollheim remembers starting the Arisians later, after the blowup described in the next chapter, as a substitute for the blown-up Futurian Society. This is my recollection too, but I found the following item in the first issue of Merril's wall newspaper, *Fouturian Home Journal,* dated February 8, 1945: "Fan, female, 6-8, personality, attractive, fill niche in Arisians. Apply Wollheim (Queens)."

I think we all tend to remember things, not in the order in which they actually happened, but in an order that makes sense.

it was very difficult to get hold of meat then, it was wartime, and I had walked *blocks* that afternoon to find a butcher who would actually sell me a couple of pounds of chopped meat, with which I had made a strange and wonderful meat loaf that was actually pretty darned good. They wouldn't eat any of it."

In March 1945 my father had had a heart attack, and I flew home to stay for a few weeks. I remember that I was bumped at every stop, and saw something (but not as much as I wanted) of the night life of Denver and Chicago. While I was gone, I heard that Merril, Kidd and Shaw had been inducted into the Futurian Society, and wrote a poem about it:

> *Three more into the fleshpots!*
> *Zissman, like a maddened Buddha,*
> *Probing her umbilicus;*
> *Emden, meditating orgies*
> *Behind a housecat's smile;*
> *Shaw, a pipe and spectacles*
> *Inhabited by vileness.*
>
> *The triumvirs annoint their swollen lips:*
> *Michel, a slow-fused pistol at his head;*
> *The turgid Lowndes, extinguishing in flesh;*
> *And Wollheim, on a roundtrip ticket to*
> *The womb. They chant their scatoliturgies,*
> *Defy the gods (with backsides shielded), and*
> *The thing is done—the Innocents are doomed!*

The reference to Judy is to her insistence on talking about belly-button flug; she had an idea that tons of it were going to waste, and that it could be used to stuff pillows or something.

In July, on a day Kidd remembers as "Black Friday," Blish told her that he loved her but had no intention of ever getting married; one word led to another, and by the end of the evening their affair was over.

Kidd wrote me about this in 1976: "On Black Friday—broken heart, hurt pride, and all that scene—tears by the gallon—I went from my front room over to Judy's, where she and Michel were in bed, and issued the Bourgeoise's Manifesto: Virginia, spurned, was going to sleep around. Judy dared me to seduce you, so I did. The brief side trip with Larry was (a) because I did not feel a 100% commitment to you, however much I liked you (a lot), and therefore my ideal of fidelity did not apply, and (b) getting Larry into bed was undertaken as loving philanthropy. The whole period lasted about one month, during which Jim and Judy became lovers briefly."

Virginia Kidd's figure, in her twenties, was plump but slim-waisted, almost like that of a John Held woman. In her sensuality there was always something motherly. "One of the reasons that Judy and I got along as well as we did," she told me, "was because I was looking for a sort of son, and she was looking for a father."

Shaw told me, "She was convinced that I had fallen in love with her, because I seemed to be looking at her breasts and knees all the time. Once she turned the lights down low, we sat on the sofa together, and she said, 'Larry, I'm aware that you're in love with me, and in a way I'm in love with you, but nothing is ever going to happen, so just forget it, it will be better for you.'

"I remember an incident when the three of us were on a bus; she was holding my hand, and you looked at her and said, 'If you're seducing me, how come you're holding hands with him?'

"Virginia had not seen any fanzines for a long time, so one evening I took her a stack of them. Chester happened to have along a copy of 'The Bastard King of England,'* and he left it in an envelope on top of that stack of fanzines. She wrote me a letter telling me off for leaving it for her to see. Then she discovered I hadn't done it, and she wrote another letter asking me not to read the first letter when it came in the mail, just to tear it up and throw it away. She was out with Lowndes that evening, and I must have been still working for *Hat Life*, because she deliberately steered the conversation onto men's straw hats, and tried to persuade Lowndes that he should buy one for the summer. Lowndes's only conception of straw hats was a flat skimmer type, and she said, 'Oh, no, there are lots of other kinds of straw hats, and Larry can tell you all about it.'

"So they appeared at our place on West 4th Street, quite late one night, and she said, 'Sorry to break in so late, but Doc and I have been talking about straw hats, and he'd like some more information.'

"So I told him about straw hats, and she slipped me this note she'd written."

The note proposed an assignation. The next day Shaw confessed to me that he didn't know what to do in bed with a woman, and I lent him a book called *Sane Sex Life and Sane Sex Living* which I had stolen from a bookstore in Portland, Oregon, in 1940.

By instinct and guesswork I had ticked off Virginia pretty well in "Three More Into the Fleshpots"—"meditating orgies behind a housecat's smile" is not bad. Virginia was flirtatious and sensuous, but also very tender-hearted and easily wounded. There was a touch of incongruous primness about her, as in the "Bastard King of England" episode, or when she

---

*A bawdy song, popularly attributed to Rudyard Kipling. The copy in question was typed, and obscenely illustrated in pencil by Cohen.

forbade Shaw to use the word "shit" in her presence, and he turned the tables by remarking, "I can't say it on you, Emden."

If the object of her brief affair with me and her even briefer one with Shaw was to make Blish jealous, it succeeded. Virginia remembers that on the evening of V-J Day, Lowndes had taken her out to dinner to propose to her again. Back at Washington Street, they found a party in progress; Blish was there, and that night he confessed that he could not bear to give her up.

The following spring Merril moved into an apartment on West 19th Street to await the return of her husband, and Blish moved into her half of Parallax, which was rechristened in the following manner. Blish began a sentence in a tough-guy accent: "The name of this jernt is—fort'wit'—" And Kidd said, "Fort Wit!"

In 1947, when Virginia was divorced from Jack Emden, she and Blish were married.

Part of Blish's early reluctance may have had something to do with the fact that he preferred kittens to children; it is not always easy for a young man to accept the role of father to a child of his wife's previous marriage. In the case of Karen Emden, I think, he did it with mixed success.

He was more than ordinarily fond of cats, and told many stories about them. Once, when a small kitten climbed up the inside of his trouser leg at Fort Wit, he discovered that the only way to get it out was to open his fly. In the midst of this operation, he glanced up and found himself being observed with fascination by a neighbor across the airshaft. The rest of the story, he admitted, was apocryphal: "And when I met her on the stairs the next day, she muttered, 'My God, ears!' "

Only once during this period, as far as I can remember, did Blish tell or write any story about children; it was a four-part fantasy about Karen Anne Emden, then in diapers; Kidd published it in her Vanguard magazine, *Discrete:*

FOUR VARIATIONS ON A WELL-KNOWN THEME

I: Maestoso

As the tall and gracious Karen Emden made her appearance upon the speaker's platform, the crowd sprang to its feet, roaring "Ungaby! Ungaby!" in a mighty collective shout, and waving a myriad of banners. The candidate smiled and waited for the uproar to subside a little, the while stepping to the rostrum; then, hitching up her diapers, she spoke . . .

II: Adagio

Ladies and gentlemen of the radio audience, I wish you could be with me to see the terrible desolation of this little Emdan town. As I drive by in my Mark III tank, I can see to one side and the other a thousand possessions scattered at random about me, and here and there the villagers squat disconsolately in the ruins of their trousers . . .

III: Marche Slav

The wind howled and moaned as little Kerensky Emdenoff went through the streets, diapers dragging, holding out a forlorn little bundle of matches. "Please, sir," she said, "won't you buy some? If I don't sell them all, my mother beats me when I get home . . ."

IV: Giocoso

As the crowds mill in the streets, a distant drone is heard in the east, and after a moment a mighty form looms on the horizon. It is the *Karen,* majestic monarch of the sky, diapers whirling, flying in tight swastika formation with itself. Thunder of approbation among the assembled Futurians.

After Blish moved out of Blowndsh, Lowndes stayed there alone for a time with a white Persian cat named Charles who stole pencils.

"Frequently at night I would open the door to come in," he said, "and there would be Charles dropping down from the top of a chair, with a long pencil in his mouth, holding it by the eraser end. And I couldn't find the pencils. But one day I moved the bed, and there was a pencil mine."

He had given his first cat, Blackout, to the Blishes. Kidd told me, "For years after that, Blackout knew when Bob was coming up the stairs, and about a flight and a half before he could have gotten to our door, Blackout would get up and go to the door and wait until Bob came in, which was astonishing to me.

"And Bob served dinners on a card table—very good dinners, specifically veal with pumpernickel stuffing, which was extraordinarily good. Charles took a deep interest in anything that was on that card table, so before Bob would put anything on it, he would open the sliding doors to the next room, and in a very dramatic way say, 'Siberia!' and throw him—you had to throw him all the way across the room in order to get the doors shut before he got back in."

The Vanguard Amateur Press Association was ingrown to begin with and got more so as time went on. There were a few outside members who contributed to the mailings, but the others were so closely associated that they tended to concen-

WORLDS BEYOND

Science-Fantasy Fiction

DECEMBER
25 CENTS

HP

SIX-LEGGED SVENGALI BY MACK REYNOLDS
& FREDRIC BROWN

GRAHAM GREENE • PHILIP WYLIE • JACK VANCE • C. M. KORNBLUTH

pebble
in the
sky

pebble
in the
sky

isaac
asimov

isaac
asimov

doubleday
science
fiction

SYNDIC

THE SYNDIC

C·M·KORNBLUTH

C.M.
KORNBLUTH

DOUBLEDAY
SCIENCE
FICTION

DOUBLEDAY SCIENCE FICTION

THE POCKET BOOK OF
SCIENCE-FICTION

EDITED BY
DONALD A. WOLLHEIM

Galaxy
SCIENCE FICTION

MAY 1951
35¢

MARS CHILD By Cyril Judd

There's somethin' the matter with me, Spike. A fellow oughtn't be able to do a thing like this...

illustration by damon knight

⭑ PATRIOTISM PLUS ⭑

Georgie Peters could create things just by concentrating on them — which was nice — only he couldn't get them right. That man he dreamed up was a pretty weird-looking duck. But Appleton of the War Department had an idea . . .

Herbert West: Reanimator

By H. P. LOVECRAFT

Here's the fourth episode in this spine-refrigerating series—in which a young scientist fights a duel to the death . . . with Death!

IV. The Scream of the Dead

THE scream of a dead man gave to me that acute and added horror of Dr. Herbert West which harrowed the latter years of our companionship. It is natural that such a thing as a dead man's scream should give horror, for it's obviously not a pleasing or ordinary occurrence; but I was used to similar experiences, hence suffered on this occasion only because of a particular circum

96

John Michel, in an illustration by Knight (*Weird Tales,* 1944).

trate on each other's work in a kind of half-oral, half-mimeo-graphed dialogue. Even the Forest Hills members were excluded from this inner circle; the rest—Blish, Kidd, Merril, Shaw, Lowndes and I—met after every mailing to discuss the contents, and these conversations fed back into the next mailing, and so on.

Even this small group developed a split, partly along political lines and partly between the serious and frivolous members. I was one of the latter; I got sucked into amateur publishing again chiefly because I was irritated by the intellectual snobbishness and pomposity of some of Blish's contributions: Blish, however, admitted errors so readily and so completely without rancor that he disarmed me, and we became close friends.

VAPA lasted for about three years before it petered out. Meanwhile, Lowndes and Blish had formed a Vanguard Record Company which actually pressed a number of records before it, too, expired.

LIKE THE REMNANTS
OF AN EXPLODED PLANETOID...

One evening in September 1945, Michel told Merril that he had to stop seeing her. Accounts of this incident differ, and one of the principal actors is dead.

SHAW: I remember distinctly that he told me he was going to break off his affair with Judy because Donald had told him to. Donald was wanting to break off relations with several people, and he wanted Johnny with him. Blish was supposed to be the worst, because at the time he was actually calling himself a fascist. That was very, very bad. But Blish was the worst, Judy and Virginia were just not much good, you and Chester were unreliable. So Johnny left, went over to Judy's; I waited a few minutes and went over to Virginia's.

MERRIL: This was the ultimatum, that it was Donald or me.

And this is why it was so painful that he should just prefer Donald to me.

KIDD: My feeling was that Donald stood in the position of a brother and a father both to him, that it never crossed his mind really to question any directive that Donald gave him. He had been struggling upstream for the past however-many weeks or months, and continuing to see you knowing that Donald disapproved.

MERRIL: Yeah, I'm sure this was true, as far as the struggling upstream, and Donald had disapproved of me for some time. And I'm sure that professional and ideological and old Futurian bonds were all connected with the fact that he did feel guilty about having an affair with me. And so, knowing that my husband would be coming home—because at that time I entertained no notion at all of breaking with my husband—Johnny may have felt that he should choose a friend he would be able to keep, rather than choosing one that he would lose in any case. He was very upset. He was not happy about doing it—I don't mean just unhappy about having to deliver a difficult message—but he was, I would guess, quite torn about it. Apparently he'd had a long discussion with Larry beforehand, trying to work his way— And I think Larry had also told him he was a shit for doing it, or something like this.

KNIGHT: Why couldn't you have kept on seeing Johnny and just not tell Donald?

MERRIL: That would have involved my agreeing to meet him in secret places or something like that, which I wouldn't have done.

SHAW: After Johnny had delivered his message and was ready to leave, he stepped into the kitchen for a minute or so and said, "I'm leaving, Larry, are you coming with me?'

And I said, "No." Then I went into Judy's apartment, went to the other end where the bedroom was, and she was sitting on the bed crying, and I comforted her.

Larry and Judy turned up at Nome shortly thereafter and recruited Chester and me for an indignation meeting at Virginia's. Late into the evening we composed a document reading Donald, Elsie and John out of the Futurian Society. Lowndes, who had resigned earlier, was talked into rejoining in order to sign the document. We cut stencils, ran them off on Larry's mimeograph, and mailed "X1" the next day to a list of s.f. fans.

A few weeks later Art Saha, a member of the Arisians, served us all with summonses: Wollheim was suing us for libel in the Supreme Court of the State of New York, and asking $25,000 damages on the ground of injury to his professional reputation.

KIDD: I remember opening the door, to someone I vaguely recognized, who asked me who I was, and I told him, and he told me who he was—Art Saha—and I asked him to come in and have a cup of coffee. He came in and sat down in the room right next to the kitchen on our side of the double apartment which was mine by then—and he had his cup of coffee, and halfway through it handed us the papers. I thought that was an abuse of hospitality, and I did not forgive that for many years. But I met Art at a convention years later: I met Taime; I was on a jury with her, of the costume ball, such as it was—there were nine judges, and I think eight contestants—and I asked her if I had heard right, that her last name was Saha, and she said, "Yes, indeed, that's my husband over there.' I told her in two phrases howcome I remembered Art; she went over and got him and brought him over, and he kissed me, and I kissed him back, and we were friends.

We went first to the Legal Aid Society, where a nervous law student fumbled through law books he had obviously never seen before and told us what to do; we did it, and got ourselves into default. Then we went to real lawyers, in a body, and I recall that while we were in one waiting room, Lowndes, wearing a red vest, told me the plot of Book Two of Tolstoy's *War and Peace,* which he had just been reading. This was a place with Colonial lintels over the doorways, and the counselor we talked to told us, with a wonderfully sincere expression on his face, that we were all in this together, etc.; but he wanted too much money. Finally we found another lawyer, who, with one phone call, got us out of default. The case was dismissed, but it still cost us $700 in lawyer's fees. We split it six ways, since Chester had no money.

> WOLLHEIM: The real history of how it broke up . . . I was getting fed up because Jim Blish was very much the reactionary as far as we were concerned. We could tolerate that, but what happened was that I decided this was all getting to be a big bore. And Michel agreed with me, but actually he was getting panicky because her husband was coming back from the South Pacific, and Judy being an enlightened woman had been writing him lurid detailed accounts of her romantic affair with Johnny Michel. He didn't think the husband would be quite as enlightened. I only found out years later that apparently when he went around to tell you people that we were breaking, he put the blame on me, that I had ordered him to do it, which is not true. He was in complete agreement, but he put the blame on me, and it was not till two years later that I found out why you people got so goddamn mad about it. Then

you people rushed out this crazy journal, and since I had made a decision not to get involved in fandom again, I was not going to put out a counter-journal, I was going to sue you to stop it.

LOWNDES: The reason why I was willing to join you was because I saw immediately this was a way I could break with Michel. As far as I was concerned John was a snake in the grass. He was a troublemaker. For some years I enjoyed John's coming over and telling me all the dirt about other people. Finally—I'm not awfully bright, Damon—it dawned on me that John was also telling other people all the dirt about me.

KNIGHT: He never gossiped much to me, that I remember.

LOWNDES: At that time, Damon, you were not of any value to him. Donald was, I was. Johnny was a smart Irishman— half Irish, half Jewish, combining the best and worst features of both. It's sad. He was so loaded with talent. He wrote a short-short story which I published, under a pen name, and Jim, who did not know who it was by, did a criticism of it and was just bowled over by it.*

---

*The story was "The Mile," by "John Tara," published in *Future Fiction,* Spring 1957. Blish wrote: " 'The Mile' . . . describes, with considerable effect, the thoughts of a baby being born only to die immediately thereafter. . . . This has been done before (most notably by Maude Hutchins) in the mainstream, and this version contains nothing which would convert the idea into a science-fiction story, but the point of view attributed to the baby—a sort of stew of mangled scraps of knowledge, philosophy and Village cynicism—is startling, despite the author's fondness for bootless tricks with clichés. If this author is a beginner—as the text suggests that he may be—he can go nowhere from this beginning but out of science fiction, and the sooner the better; he is too good even raw to be bothered with a protracted adolescence at wonder-mongering."

In the second volume of his collected essays, *More Issues At Hand* (Advent, 1970), Blish added a note: "Lowndes tells me that 'Tara' was the well-known science-fiction fan and sometime author (mostly as 'John Raymond' [sic: it was Hugh Raymond]), John B. Michel. I think my jaw must have hung open for at least two days after this revelation."

Don told me later, after we got together again, that the reason he entered suit was not to collect money from us; just to stop it from going any farther. The whole thing was handled so badly on our part. I now and then just wonder where I'd be now if, at a time like that, I'd taken a different turn.

Looking back, you can sometimes see that people have been in a repeating pattern for years without knowing it. Will Sykora cast out those members of the International Scientific Association whose views he thought dangerous; the expelled members, led by Wollheim, dissolved the organization and left Sykora stranded. Eight years later Wollheim made exactly the same mistake, with almost the same results. The Futurian Society was not officially dissolved, but it never met formally again, and there was a tacit understanding after a few months that it was dead.

Patterns are not easy to kill. Like the remnants of an exploded planetoid, the Futurians were hurled away from a common center in orbits that repetitively intersected for years.

In 1948 Lowndes met and married a woman named Dorothy (later Barbara) Rogalin, who had a young son from a previous marriage. They stayed in Lowndes's West 11th Street apartment awhile, then moved up to the Riverdale section of the Bronx for a year. They returned to West 11th Street, then bought a house in Suffern, New York, where they stayed eleven years. In 1965 they moved to a co-op on Fifth Avenue at 108th Street. In 1967 they agreed to separate.

"The plan was that Dorothy and I would get separate apartments, and that I would show my good faith by getting one first; and I found this place in Hoboken, but we wound up with Dorothy moving in with me here." She finally left, and they were amicably divorced in 1974.

"Dorothy was a henpecker," Kidd told me. "She was kind of pretty, and small—and belittled him at every turn—there was nothing he could do right. She would apologize for him, and explain that Bob couldn't do this or that, because Bob just wasn't competent.

"However, I ordered a wooden table from Sears and Roebuck, with drop leaves on the ends and a narrow center section, with three little drawers on each side—because the Lowndeses had had one, and it was utterly convenient—open it up and you could seat six or in a pinch, eight people at this table, and when you closed it up you had something very small and narrow, up against the wall. And when it arrived, it was a put-it-together-yourself piece of furniture, and Jim absolutely refused to tackle it, until I told him Dorothy had told me that Bob had put theirs together, and Jim said, 'If Bob can do it, I can do it'—and he did.

"It wasn't all that difficult; I could have done it too."

In 1948 Shaw, Cohen and I took an apartment together in Little Italy; it had a living room and two bedrooms, but no kitchen; I don't remember that this struck any of us as odd. We called the place "the Cell." The first night there, our furniture had not been delivered yet, and Cohen, his brother Eddie and I slept on the floor until about three in the morning, when we were awakened by a flashlight shining in our eyes. Somebody must have reported suspicious-looking characters, and a policeman had come up to see if we were burglars or junkies or what.

It was here that Shaw threw a fan named Sam Mason down the stairs because he wanted his bed back. Mason had been living in the tenement adjoining Shaw's on West 17th Street. The building was unheated, Shaw remembers, "and it was a bitterly cold winter, so he more or less moved in with me for a while, bringing his bed with him, and I just took it along when I moved; I didn't bother to tell him where we were for a while. So one day he came up demanding his bed, pounding on the door and yelling, and since your mother was there visiting at the time, I wanted to get rid of him quickly, so I pushed him down the stairs." Shaw sent the bed back later, by "some sort of freight collect."

By this time Blish had gone broke trying to write for a living and was working as a reader for the Scott Meredith Literary Agency. He got me an interview there and they gave me a test manuscript to criticize. I remember that I flunked the first time, but for some reason they let me try again later and hired me.

Kidd told me, "When Jim worked for Scott Meredith, during the latter part of the period he was ill with nicotine poisoning, and didn't know it—he was getting sicker every day, and was having more and more trouble getting through the amount of work he was supposed to do. He developed a nicotine allergy, or something—and he brought home two or three letters a night, because he couldn't do the six he was supposed to do at work—and I did them, which is where I learned the plot skeleton—and actually where I learned much of what I know from the pulp side of how to write."

At Meredith's I met a buxom nineteen-year-old blonde, Trudy Werndl, and after a few months we were married. We moved out to Staten Island to share a house with Jim and Virginia, and for a while Jim and I grew as fat as we were ever likely to get, because Trudy and Virginia took turns in the kitchen, and it developed into a cooking contest in which Virginia held her own, even though Jim had quit his job to free-lance again, and they were broke.

One evening after work, Blish, Trudy and I went out for a

drink. The three of us were sitting at the bar, Trudy in the middle. A Navy officer sitting beside Blish made some offensive remark to Trudy which I did not hear, and Blish slapped him in the face. Instead of laying Jim out with an uppercut to the jaw, as he would have done if this had been a movie, the officer slapped him in return, breaking his glasses. Out on the street a few minutes later, Blish said piteously, "I don't know what I'm going to tell Virginia."

Jim was attracted by Germanic culture, and had either told Virginia or allowed her to think that he had traveled in Germany before the war. He had an army friend, Maximilian Knoecklein, a former Hitler Youth, with whom he spent beery evenings, singing German drinking songs. Virginia remembers the night Munich was bombed, "when Maxl walked with us around Greenwich Village throwing imaginary grenades; I believe he was crying, or close to it."

Knoecklein married an army nurse, "and during the worst of the poverty that Jim and I lived through, they supplied us with bags of rice that were intended for refugees somewhere else. One sack of rice lasted for months, during that period when we had thirty-three cents to last us for three months, and our credit slowly ran out with the local grocer. That was the same period when I scavenged out of the garbage half a dozen less than perfect brussels sprouts that Trudy had thrown out as not good enough to cook for you."

A little later Trudy got appendicitis and I got cerebrospinal meningitis, and after a while we and the Blishes found that we were getting on each other's nerves. Our marriage was going downhill, too, and Trudy and I moved into a studio apartment in the Village to see if that would help, but it didn't.

During this period I saw almost nothing of the Futurians. Cohen had shipped out as a yeoman, i.e. a seagoing clerk-typist, and after a few crossings had jumped ship in England where he lived with an English girl for three months. He told me later that he had lent some copies of *Astounding* to his landlord, who brought them back a week later and said confidentially, "It's *all lies,* y'know."

Shaw also shipped out once as a messman on a Liberty ship, but disliked it so much that on the return voyage he managed to break his glasses; being unable to see the plates or the tables, he was relieved of duty.

In 1949 I did another stint as a reader at Scott Meredith's, where I so perfected my aim with a wad of paper that I could pot Don Fine or James A. Bryans across the room, sitting or standing. Bryans later became editor-in-chief of a paperback company, Popular Library; Fine now has his own trade publishing company, Arbor House.

When I left Meredith's after a few months, I helped Shaw get a job there. By that time Lester del Rey had joined the agency as a reader and had become a sort of unofficial office manager. Others who worked for Meredith during Shaw's time were Evan Hayman and Walter Fultz, both of whom later became paperback editors. Shaw remembers that it was Fultz who discovered Richard Prather, a highly successful writer of hard-boiled mysteries. Prather had sent in a reading-fee manuscript which Fultz immediately saw was publishable, but he was in a quandary whether to recommend it to Meredith or not, because if Meredith had turned it down, Fultz would have failed to make his quota for the week. He took the risk, and the rest is royalty statements.

Wollheim kept looking for opportunities and finding them. In 1942 Pocket Books, the first American paperback publisher, was issuing a series of books with such titles as *The Pocket Book of*

Westerns, The Pocket Book of Detective Stories, etc. Wollheim proposed a *Pocket Book of Science Fiction,* and to his surprise they bought it. It was the first paperback anthology of science fiction—still one of the best—and the first to use "science fiction" in its title. Later, when Viking had begun to issue their "Portable Novels" series, Wollheim persuaded them to do *The Portable Novels of Science Fiction.* For Avon he did the *Avon Fantasy Reader* series on a fee basis—they bought the stories he selected, and paid him $100 a volume.

"Then after about the second or third issue had appeared, Herb Williams [of Avon] called me up and said, 'I want to hire an assistant editor to work with me.' And I said to myself, well, this sounds like a good idea, I think pocketbooks have a future, and whether they do or not, I'm not going to have a future [at Ace] if Matt Phillips reclaims his job.

"And I was working there about two or three months, I came in one morning, and Herb said to me, 'Look, over the weekend we had a long discussion and family fight, and my mother's leaving the company, and I'm going to leave with her. From now on you're going to have to be the editor.'

"And from that point on I was the editor, chief copy editor, cook, bottle-washer, first reader and everything else, being the only person in the editorial department. I think they did about six titles a month, and they did one of these digest-sized books a month, sometimes two. People would approach Joe Myers with a crazy idea, and he'd try it. I was the editor of a big slick magazine for about three years, some kind of a cheesy confessions-true-love thing with photographs—*Love Stories,* or some idiot title—it was not pornography, you know, just *smutty.*"

Wollheim's job at Avon lasted five years, "the five most miserable years" of his life. During this period Wollheim came down with appendicitis, was released from the hospital after a week, and three days later went back in with a lung embolism; he spent two and a half months in intensive care.

"During that period Joe [Myers] was very decent about it, although he was still no fun to work for. Eventually things got so bad that I made a couple of efforts to leave the place, and was interviewed at Dell at one point; nothing came of that; and I got the idea of approaching A. A. Wyn—I knew he had always wanted to go into books."

A. A. Wyn liked the idea of starting a line of paperbacks, but he hated to make up his mind. Several months passed, and meanwhile Wollheim was interviewed for an assistant editor's job at Pyramid Books.

"And they made a classic mistake. They called Rose Wyn to get my credentials, they wanted a reference. And I never worked for Rose Wyn—she handled the love pulps—but she told Aaron, and Aaron jumped through the sky, and called me up on Friday and said, 'Come down at once.' I went down to his office Friday afternoon and he hired me on the spot."

Between them, Wyn and Wollheim founded Ace Books, for many years a highly successful publishing operation. Among their innovations were the Ace Double Novels—two short novels published back to back in the same binding, each upside down with reference to the other.

Judith Merril and her husband took up residence together on West 19th Street in 1946 but separated a few months later. In her divorce action I found myself testifying before a referee named Schmuck* that Judy's husband and a blond woman had

---

*Schmuck, in German, means "treasure," but in Yiddish slang it is the equivalent of the English "prick." There is a story, which may be true, about a citizen who came before Schmuck with a petition to change his name from

used one of the bedrooms in my apartment for immoral purposes. (Under New York law at that time adultery was the only
ground for divorce.)

The referee, a white-haired old man who looked like a
vulture, asked me, "What were you running, a whorehouse?"
and frequently muttered, "There'll be no divorce in this case,
no divorce." In the end he granted it.

Pohl's marriage to Dorothy Les Tina broke up in 1948.
She had written a novel, *Occupation: Housewife* (published by
Morrow in 1949) and Pohl says she was "much more career-
minded" than he was willing to put up with. "She was also
deathly opposed to having children, and while I wasn't particularly convinced either way, I didn't like having the option
foreclosed. And we got along quite well most of the time, but
somewhat to my surprise she went to California in 1948, and I
got a letter from her saying, 'The weather is very nice here and
my mother is fine, and by the way, I've filed suit for divorce.' "

It was shortly after this that Lowndes brought Pohl over to
Merril's apartment. Merril remembers that evening very well.
"Of course I had heard a lot of mythic stories about Fred,
'Sixty-forty Pohl' and all this; and Bob brought Fred over and
brought a bottle of vodka, and they sat in front of the fireplace
and proceeded to have a vodka drinking contest. There was a
good deal of conversation in the early part of the evening, in
which I was very interested, and I found Fred strange, interesting—not at that point attractive, but interesting, and I wanted
the conversation to go on, but it failed fairly rapidly in view of
this vodka drinking contest. And, I mean, they were quite
serious about it, they finished the bottle, and we got another

---

Lipschitz to Collins. The judge told him, *"My* name is Schmuck. My *father's*
name was Schmuck. My *grandfather's* name was Schmuck," etc.

bottle from Margaret next door, which was about half full, and they went on with the contest. And Bob won, by a narrow margin, that is to say, with one drink left in the bottle, Fred collapsed unconscious on the couch. Bob triumphantly took the last drink and staggered out the door, leaving me with Fred, who got up the next morning and made his exit as quickly as possible.

"The next time I met Fred was at a convention in Philadelphia, where *I* got drunk—it was one of the memorable few times that I got completely stinking polluted drunk. I will add a joke even though it has nothing to do with the Futurians, just for your delectation. Waiting for a performance that was going to be put on, in which Sturgeon and Mary Mair were going to be singing, I was sitting in the second or third row, and somebody behind me tapped my shoulder and said, 'Do you know where it's possible to get a drink around here?' And I asked the person on the right, and the person on the left, and then tapped the person in front of me and said, 'Do you know where it's possible to get a drink around here on Sunday?' And this guy turned around with this long face and looked at me, and he said, 'My name is George O. Smith and I *always* know where it's possible to get a drink. And *you* may join me.'

"Anyhow, at this convention, I had meant to go just for the day, but it looked like a pretty good party, and I wanted to stay overnight. So I asked Phil Klass if he had any money—you needed five bucks for the hotel room—and Phil didn't have any, and I couldn't see anyone else I knew around. And then Fred wandered by, and although I barely knew him, I figured, I really wanted to stay—he looked like somebody who had some money, so I tapped him and said, 'Have you got five dollars you can lend me for a hotel room?'

"And he said, 'Sure I do,' and gave it to me, and I got my room. And then that evening was when I got uproariously, joyously, gloriously drunk. I was going around to four different rooms where things were going on. In one of those rooms (it was still Sunday in Philadelphia, you understand) there was Hadley [a publisher], who had a big booze party going on, and it was the last booze there was in the hotel that anyone could find. And then there were two other parties, and then there was a room where people were playing poker. And both Fred and Phil were in the poker game. So with great sentimental attachment to the man who had lent me the money to stay, and my old buddy Phil, I would include the poker game in my rounds, and I would go sit on Phil's lap and help him with his cards, and he would get rid of me as quickly as possible, and then I would go on, and I was making the rounds of these four places regularly. There was a college fraternity convention also going on at that hotel, and by the time I would arrive at the Hadley party each time, I would have a following of eight or ten college students, to whom I had been saying, *'Sure,* I know where there's something to drink.' I would be carefully segregated from them, and taken into the room, and they would be banished, and after a while I would disappear and go back to the poker game.

"It was also during that evening that I first met John Campbell. One of my few snapshot memories of that evening, after really starting to drink, is standing in a bedroom in somebody's hotel suite with my hand on John Campbell's shoulder and his hand on mine, saying to him, 'John, I wrote a story 'at's so good, ish mush too good for you.' And he said, 'You're right. If'sh that good, we don' pay enough for it.'

"Anyhow, there came a point where I suddenly started to feel very ill. And I must have been in the vicinity of the poker game at the time, because Mort Klass [Phil's younger brother] was there also, and Mort took me up to my room and put me to bed.

"The next time I met Fred, somewhere else—it may have been at the founding meeting of the Hydra Club, or something like that—I gave him back the five dollars, and then a few days after that he called up and asked me to go out with him. During that evening he said he was fascinated, because when he gave me the five dollars he had expected to sleep with me, and I had gotten so rotten drunk nobody could think about it, but the *last* thing he had expected was that I would give him back the five dollars."

The story Merril refers to is "That Only a Mother," which Campbell did publish and which made Merril's reputation in science fiction. The Hydra Club was formed in the late forties by nine people ("some of whom never showed up again")—hence the name. The moving spirits included Pohl, Merril and Lester del Rey.

Presently Pohl moved into Merril's apartment on East 4th Street, and two years later they were married, partly because they wanted to have a child. This was Ann, now in her twenties, who made Pohl a grandfather in 1973.

Harry Dockweiler came back from the war with the same disease that had killed Michel's mother, tuberculosis of the spine; it is not clear whether this had anything to do with his jeep accident, but Rosalind's uncle, a lawyer, succeeded in getting him a small pension.

> POHL: For a year or so he was trying to get a job, or trying to make up his mind what to do with his life. But he was in pain most of the time, and he couldn't really work. So I suggested to him that he be a literary agent, and he said, "Fine. What do I know about being a literary agent?" I said, "Nothing to it, you can do the Scott Meredith reading-fee bit." So he said, "Okay, tell me how to do it."
>
> I was working for *Popular Science* at the time. So I said,

"Tell you what I'll do, I'll help you write a sales letter to send out to writers; I'll tell you where to get the names of the writers, from the slush pile of Popular Publications." [Popular, like other large chain publishers, kept the envelopes in which unsolicited manuscripts were received and sold them, with their return addresses, as mailing lists.] "And if you want to know anything else that I know, I'll tell you."

So he did, and I wrote him a letter and he sent it out, and he got a lot of reading-fee manuscripts in. And one or two fairly promising pulp writers, mostly Western writers. So he began trying to peddle their stuff, under the name of Dirk Wylie Literary Agents, and he sold one or two stories. And then he began getting sicker, and he couldn't deal with the correspondence, so I began answering his letters for him.

ROSALIND: He was home for a long time, and he was trying to write; he was up in my grandmother's house, which was two stories above my house—it was a four-story duplex house in Brooklyn, and she had given him a room up there. But he was getting sicker all the time. He wouldn't let me call a doctor, but finally he took to his bed—he couldn't walk. And my godfather is a doctor, and he just happened to be in the house that night. He found an abscess on his back and decided he'd have to go into the hospital. So they put him into Adelphi Hospital and they opened this up, and they discovered that he had a tubercular condition.

Finally my godfather had him put into St. Albans Naval Hospital, where he just went downhill for another year. And they put him into a cast from his lower chest down— and his legs were spread out, with a bar between them. That's the way that guy lay for over a year.

He wanted very badly to go to Lourdes. I didn't know any way of getting him to Lourdes. At one point we were going to bring him home for the Christmas holidays—he must have been living for that day. About a day before, there was a tremendously heavy snowstorm, and it was just impossible. That was the blizzard of '48.* After that, it was just all the way down, and fast. He died in August.

POHL: When he died, he was down to eighty-five pounds. And Roz wanted to continue the agency, and I said, "Okay, let's do it as a partnership." And we did, and then I quit my job at *Popular Science* and went into being an agent full time.

ROSALIND: The first office we ever had was in Dick Wilson's home and office, which was on 46th Street between Lexington and Third avenues. There was a row of houses there, and after he decided to move out, we moved in. The amazing thing is that they ultimately tore down that entire square block, and they put up 750 Third Avenue, which is where my office was located fifteen years later. I mean Dell moved into that building. [Rosalind later became, and still is, associate editor of the Dell puzzle magazines.] And then Dick Wilson went to work for Transradio Press, and he was letting me be women's reporter for Transradio. I was covering things like breakfasts, style shows. I would write this little squib and Dick would rewrite it down to four words. Transradio Press was on Fifth Avenue between 43rd and 44th streets. They were up in the penthouse, and Dick got us a little room up there, from which we operated.

---

*I was married to Trudy in that blizzard—we were two hours late getting to the church, and the minister gave us a cold eye.

POHL: I began trying to attract better clients, and I got a lot of science fiction writers. And I sold a lot of science fiction —most of what was being bought, as a matter of fact. Campbell bought more than half of everything he bought from me; so did Horace [Gold], and so did most of the major publishers. When Doubleday came in I helped them set up the line, and they bought most of the first few books from me.

ASIMOV: And of course Fred was instrumental in getting my first book published. Because he was the one who came to me and told me that Doubleday needed books, and I said I didn't have anything, and he said, "What about the story you wrote for *Startling Stories* last summer," that had been rejected by *Startling* after they'd ordered it, and I passed it on to John Campbell and he rejected it, and I said, convinced by the rejections, "No, it stinks." And he said, "Let 'em look it over at least." So I promised I would bring it over to his place, and he would take it in to Doubleday as my agent. And I brought it over. And at that time he was married to Judy Merril, and Judy had an eight-year-old daughter by a previous marriage, and the daughter was the only one home when I came. I don't remember whether I came at the wrong time or what. I suspect, because I wasn't indignant, that I had just come over without warning. Anyway, so little did I think of this story that I handed the manuscript to an eight-year-old girl and said, "Give this to your father when he comes back."

This was Asimov's *Pebble in the Sky;* Doubleday offered him a $250 option and asked him to revise and expand it to 70,000 words, and he did.

After that, Asimov says, he couldn't very well not have

Fred as his agent, even though he was always uncomfortable working with an agent.

> POHL: I developed this plan of how to get writers to write, which was that I would give them a check when they turned in a manuscript, without even reading it—which had the effect on many writers, present company included, of making them write a great deal more and a great deal better than they ever had before. The only thing was that when I guessed wrong, I found myself running out of money. There was a fellow named George Kull in California [he wrote as "Dean Evans"] who wrote pretty good light mysteries, but he wrote them in enormous volume, and I couldn't sell them as fast as he wrote them—he was starving to death, and he was into me for like three thousand dollars when I wrote him off."

After the war Dick Wilson, who had divorced Jessica while he was in the service, went to Chicago and lived with his mother and brother while he attended classes at the University. Kornbluth, who had married Mary Byers before he went into the army, was also in Chicago, attending University College on a master's program.

I told Wilson that several people had talked to me about Kornbluth's cruelty; he immediately responded with an anecdote about his kindness.

Wilson was living on the "fifty-two twenty club"—$20 a week for fifty-two weeks—and he had convinced the Veterans Administration that he was a writer.

"So I was sitting there in the house one day trying to write something. And Cyril came in, and said, 'What are you doing? Why don't we go to the zoo?' And I said, 'I can't. I got to write.'

"He said, 'How much do you have to write?'

" 'I should write a couple pages today, anyway.'

"So he sat down at the typewriter and thought for a minute, and then he batted out two and a half pages of something—the beginning of a science fiction story—and said, 'There. Now you're done. Come on.'

"Anyhow, I was getting fifty dollars a month or whatever it was in addition to tuition, and living with my mother, so I looked around for a job. And I tried to get back with Fairchild Publications, because they had a Chicago office, but they weren't hiring. So somehow or other I found a small wire service with an office in Chicago—its headquarters were in New York—and they hired me as a rewrite man for twenty hours a week. I forget what I got—dollar an hour, something like that.

"And I was working twenty-thirty hours a week; it came to the point where I was getting Ds in school, and I had to decide between the job and school. So I gave up school after a year, and later Cyril came in as a rewrite man.

"We did a lot of monitoring of newscasts in those days; we did have some legitimate sources, but we did what was called 'processing the news for radio.' You can't copyright news, it's in the public domain: you can only copyright the form of words, so we would tune in and catch the latest newscasts, and often we were very good about updating the stuff—used the long-distance telephone quite a bit.

"Let's say there was a tornado in Kansas. Well, we'd place a call to the operator in that town and say, 'Can you tell us who knows about this tornado—is the chief of police around, or is there a doctor, or somebody at the hospital that you know?' And more often than not we would be in touch with an eyewitness, and get a good legitimate fresh story. And we'd feed it onto the wire. Our clients were often poor radio stations, which couldn't afford the AP or the UPI.

"So Cyril came in about that time, and when I left he took

over as bureau manager. He was a terrific writer, as you know, and he used this facility in writing news.

"The Mexico City man was also a stringer for *Variety,* and somebody had given him a hold-down on the amount of copy he could file, because it came collect at cable rates, so he would send us very tight 'cablese' copy, and Cyril would expand this, drawing liberally on his knowledge of Mexico, and his imagination—and out of a twelve- or fifteen-word cable he would produce a hundred-word story, about Bandit Attack, or Bus Falling into Ravine, or Terrible Storm, or something like that. Of course flying saucers came along at around that time. And our Mexico City man was very good about filing flying saucer stories, and Cyril had a terrific holiday with this.

"Cyril was liked and respected for his industry and talent—he was a hell of a fast writer. We had a teletype operator named George who was very calm. Cyril would sometimes get excited when he had a hot item, a bulletin or a flash, and George would say to him, 'Have you got a *bewletin,* Cyreal?'

"We were one end of a race wire there, and you can read about that in Cyril's book *The Syndic.* It was a legitimate operation, but we generally beat the official race wire. AP and UPI sent these results on the wire, and they still do it today, when the official sign flashed. Well, we had people with binoculars on high buildings overlooking the track, and we would have at least the winner, maybe not the two-three, a minute or half a minute before the official sign had been flashed. And I do believe there were some people who subscribed to our service who were not newspapers or radio stations."

In 1949 Merril wrote her first novel, *Shadow on the Hearth;* it is a story of America under the threat of atomic war, seen from the not-very-well-informed viewpoint of a young housewife and mother. (The heroine's husband, who is offstage until he makes his way home in the last chapter, is named John

Mitchell.) Doubleday published it in 1950, and it was later dramatized on TV as "Atomic Attack." Compact Books in England reprinted the novel in the sixties, but it did not appear in this country in paperback, because no one could figure out how to package it; it was neither science fiction nor women's fiction, but something in between.

Early in 1950 Merril started what she intended to be a short story, based on a fragment of Pohl's, which eventually became the *Galaxy* serial *Mars Child.* "It grew out of all proportion, and I bogged down at about eighteen thousand words when I was dumb-and-pregnant that summer. After Ann was born, I pulled it out again, and was trying to figure out which way to do it, when Cyril showed up on a week's holiday. This was at East 4th Street, before the move to Red Bank. I asked him for suggestions; he read it, asked if he could try doing something with it. I said sure. He went to the typewriter and after thirty hours or so emerged with about twenty-five or thirty thousand words, including many changes and enriching additions, constituting about half of a novel."

Merril and Kornbluth worked out a general outline for the rest and agreed to collaborate by mail after Cyril went back to Chicago. "Fred, a trifle overconfidently, sold it to Horace Gold sometime before it was finished. Horace, more overconfidently than that, began publishing it before it was done. Suddenly there was a crisis, because the first installment had been published, the second was set in type, and Cyril and I had just realized that it was going to be four installments long— Horace was expecting only three.

"So I went out to Chicago for a week to work with Cyril and see what we could figure out. He was working at the wire service then, so we would hold a big session in the evening, and he would write at night, and I would write while he was at work. One evening I went over to the Leibers', while Cyril was doing his stint, and when I came back, Cyril was sitting with a bottle of green Chartreuse at the far end of the room—it was this great big sort of storefront they were living in—there was this long table that people used for other purposes, with dishes and sculpture and other things around the edges. And Cyril was up at the far end of the table, leaning over his bottle of green Chartreuse: '*There* she is, the little mother of science fiction.' He didn't like the work I had done."

Shortly afterward the Pohls moved into a huge three-story Victorian house in Red Bank, New Jersey, where Fred still lives. The house was really more than they could afford; the agency was not showing a profit, and the marriage was deteriorating.

POHL: Judy was determined that we get out of East 4th Street. We bought this house, and I had to come up with the down payment, which was a couple thousand dollars, and the expenses of moving, all that other stuff. And I was overcommitted, I didn't have enough money to deal with it. It was annoying, because the agency was prospering, I was selling more stuff all the time, and markets were opening up and writers were writing, and I was just running out of scratch.

And I began trying to make money on the side, to subsidize the operation. I did a bunch of books for *Popular Science* for five hundred bucks each, the sort of thing I'd done when I'd been working for them—pasting up tearsheets from the magazines to be made into one-shot paperbacks.

He also began work on a novel, using the advertising background he had acquired after his disastrous first novel, but this time projecting it into a future in which the world is controlled by adman techniques. He bogged down after twenty thousand words or so, but showed what he had to H. L. Gold, who was anxious to see the work finished and suggested that he find a collaborator. Pohl chose Kornbluth, who rewrote the first part of the novel and added a middle section; then the two took turns writing the last section.

Gold published the novel in three parts in *Galaxy*, as "Gravy Planet"; it later appeared in book form as *The Space Merchants*. It has since been translated into twenty languages. Today it reads with astonishing freshness, with its "Consie" (Conservationist) underground organization, its water and food shortages, its overpopulation, its "pedicabs" and its aggressive advertising for such products as Kiddiebutt, Coffiest, and PregNot.

This passage, from page 6 of the paperback edition, sets the tone:

> "Good morning," Fowler said, and the eleven of us made the usual idiot murmur. He didn't sit down; he stood gazing paternally at us for about a minute and a half. Then, with the air of a day-tripper in Xanadu, he looked carefully and delightedly about the room.
>
> "I've been thinking about our conference room," he said, and we all looked around at it. The room isn't big, it isn't small: say ten by twelve. But it's cool, well lighted, and most imposingly furnished. The air recirculators are cleverly hidden behind animated friezes; the carpeting is thick and soft; and every piece of furniture is constructed from top to bottom of authentic, expertized, genuine tree-grown wood.

The book is a satire, published in 1952, of the anti-conservationists of the seventies:

. . . The Conservationists were fair game, those wild-eyed zealots who pretended modern civilization was in some way "plundering" our planet. Preposterous stuff. Science is *always* a step ahead of the failure of natural resources. After all, when real meat got scarce, we had soyaburgers ready. When oil ran low, technology developed the pedicab.

During this period the Pohls had a summer house in Ashokan, where Kornbluth came to visit them from Chicago.

Pohl said, "He was just east on a visit, and for one reason or another I was busy and tired, and I didn't feel like drinking. Cyril and Judy were sitting around drinking, and finally Cyril talked me into having a drink. And then he talked me into having another drink, and then I talked him into having another drink, and we got pretty fucking blind drunk. And we went out in the woods for some purpose not now known to me, and I passed out. I thought I'd got back to our house, but it turned out I had passed out in our landlady's house, which had a double Dutch door very much like ours. Threw up all over her living room. And the next day the well failed, and there was no water to flush the toilet, or take a bath or anything.

"We had a sort of complex with four or five houses up on the top of a hill over the Ashokan Reservoir, and the neighbors came over to our house to consult about what we were going to do about the well, and I was terribly hung over, drinking ginger ale one sip every hour. And I remember them saying, 'There must have been some hunters lost in the woods last night, we could hear them calling to each other.'

"When Cyril came out here, he'd drink everything in the house. I gave up buying alcoholic extracts of flavoring, because he'd drink them. His favorite drink was elixir of turpin hydrate and codeine, which was a prescription-free cough medicine, and you could make a pretty good drink out of it."

I remarked that the stuff is supposed to be habit-forming, and Pohl said, "We drank a lot of it, and I haven't felt any withdrawal symptoms; it's been twenty years. I got some a couple of years ago from my doctor when I had a hacking cough, and he cautioned me about it, and I told him I'd had more of that stuff than he'd ever seen.

"Cyril was a very heavy drinker. He drank almost all the time when he wasn't working. When he finished working at night, he'd head out for a bar and sit around drinking until he could go to sleep. I don't think he drank during the day, and he didn't drink while he was working, but when he was through for the day, he drank as much as he could hold."

The Kornbluths' first apartment in Chicago was near the stockyards. Wilson says the odor from the yards was terrible, but Kornbluth claimed he didn't smell it because the Wrigley chewing gum factory was between him and it, and the odors cancelled each other out.

"I remember them spreading Kem-Tone all over everything," Wilson told me. "I said, 'Don't you want to get the dust and grime away first?' 'Naw.' Just painted right over it and covered everything up."

Later the Kornbluths moved to the Chicago equivalent of Greenwich Village, at the lake end of 55th Street, where they lived in a storefront apartment in a row of handicraft shops. One of their neighbors, a glass engraver, appeared as a character in Kornbluth's "The Mindworm." Mary became interested in ceramics here, and this experience turned up as background material in Kornbluth's "The Marching Morons."

Kornbluth stayed on as bureau chief in Chicago for about a year after Wilson left, then went to Red Bank and lived with the Pohls, where he and Mary had a vertical three-room suite, one room on each of the three floors. Mary was pregnant, and because of a danger of miscarriage she had to spend most of her time lying down. Kornbluth and Merril were collaborating on another novel, *Gunner Cade,* which Campbell bought. It was a skillfully constructed man-who-learns-better anti-utopia, somewhat like Kornbluth's later "That Share of Glory" in tone.

Merril told me, "It was the year that we were all incredibly broke, and that many other distasteful things were happening —but for a while Cyril and Mary and Jack and Lois [Gillespie] were living there—Fred was not home much. Then Fred was home less and less; Jack and Lois had left, and Kay MacLean came for a visit—Cyril and Mary were still there—and Kate and Cyril and ᵀ got into a discussion one day. It was an all-day discussion—hours and hours and hours. It began with Cyril's objecting to my habit of allowing my eight-year-old daughter to run around the house with nothing but her underpants on. And I could not believe that he was seriously objecting to this—I was upset at the fact that she would not allow herself to appear anywhere *without* her underpants. I simply couldn't imagine what he was talking about, and Kate was equally flabbergasted, so we engaged him in conversation on this matter, and I can remember two high points from this—one of which was in the middle of it, after two or three hours; we were finishing a meal in the kitchen and Kate said to Cyril, 'You know, when I was in college I believed in free love, but I seemed never to have any opportunity to practice it. Then when I left college I began to find opportunities to try it out, and you know, I *still* believe in free love.'

"Much later, several hours later, we were up on the top floor, and Kate said to Cyril, 'To hear you talk, you might think that you had been born fully clothed,' and Cyril said, 'I certainly was,' and left the room."

———————

Pohl dissolved the Dirk Wylie agency in 1953. "For the first six months of '53 it showed an operating net profit, above all expenses, of about a hundred dollars a week, which was subsistence money. And having attained that, I folded it. I had just run out of steam. I owed a lot of money, and it was hard for me to see how to get out of debt while I was doing that. It took me ten years to pay everybody off. I paid writers off in less time than that, but there were things like the Internal Revenue. They finally caught up with me in 1965. The IRS agent said, 'How could you not file a return for seventeen years?'

"I said, 'I didn't have any money.'

"He said, 'But didn't you know you would be in trouble?' and I said, 'Yeah, I knew I'd be in trouble, but I was *already* in trouble.'

"So fortunately, that was when some idiot in England bought the film rights to *The Space Merchants* for fifty grand. All the things I've done because I knew there was a mint in them have bombed. The things I do for love sometimes pay off very well."

Asimov told me, "There was a little hard feeling between me and Fred because of a financial matter in which I felt I had been slightly cheated, but which in the end turned out to be to my benefit. What happened was, he said he needed money to stay in business, and I said, 'Well, keep the check that Horace Gold's going to send me for *Caves of Steel,* only make sure to pay me back, because Gertrude doesn't like me lending out money, and if you don't pay me back I'll be in deep trouble.'

"Anyway, he couldn't pay me back, and in fact he went out of business immediately after that. And I felt as if he hadn't been quite open with me, and I suppose that if he had been he wouldn't have got the money from me. Anyway, it was quite obvious after a while that I wasn't going to get the money back, and I didn't know what to do. There was no way in the world I could sue him. In the first place I didn't want to, because he was my friend; in the second place if I had sued him I would have looked awfully bad in the science fiction fraternity; in the third place if I sued him and didn't care how I looked, I wouldn't get a cent out of him anyway. So I remember asking Doubleday, what does one do in a case like this? And they said, 'Easy—he's your agent, ask him in return for the money, to hand back the seven book contracts that he has and not collect the ten percent anymore,' which otherwise, whether he's your agent or not, you pay for the rest of your life.* And so I figured, well, there's no way in the world in which the ten percents on those books are going to come to three thousand bucks, but something is better than nothing. But as it happened, those seven books included *Pebble in the Sky, Currents of Space, Caves of Steel, I, Robot,* and the three Foundation books. And the ten percent on what they've made me since then is—I don't know, it could easily be ten times those three thousand. So it's the other way around now. When I think of it, I feel very guilty. I feel, you know, I've got my return with an incredible number of percent interest."

With the habit of collaboration established, Pohl and Kornbluth did six more novels together in the next six years. In one of these, *A Town Is Drowning,* written after Pohl's divorce, there is a bitter portrait of a woman writer who is unmistakably Merril. I assumed this part of the book was

---

*Pohl says it was he, not Doubleday, who made this suggestion.

Pohl's, but Kornbluth told me later that he himself had written it. He and Merril had not parted on friendly terms.

Merril told me, "Cyril chose to take an extremely moralistic view of my break with Fred—he gave me a very heavy lecture at one point about the 'copybook virtues'—his phrase—and my failure to have them, and loyalty, and things like that, and I agreed with him that I did not have these 'copybook virtues.' "

In 1949 I went back to work at Popular Publications, this time under Ejler Jakobsson, who had taken over Alden Norton's department when Norton became a vice-president. I shared a large airy room with Hank Levinson, a cheerful young man whom Jakobsson had hired from the Columbia University placement bureau, and Mary Gnaedinger. Mary had the love pulps, *Famous Fantastic Mysteries,* and *Fantastic Novels;* I worked on *Super Science* (revived in 1949), and Hank and I did the Westerns, sports, and detectives between us.

Mary Gnaedinger was a placid, ladylike woman, handsome in spite of her Garden Club figure and a little too much makeup; she did her work and watched without comment while Hank and I bombarded each other with rubber-tipped darts and paper airplanes.

That winter, when my marriage to Trudy broke up, I learned that Lester's and Helen del Rey's had broken up too, and began seeing Helen. After a few months I got rid of the Waverly Place apartment and moved in with her. Working as Jakobsson's assistant on *Super Science* exasperated me; I wanted a magazine of my own, and asked Fred Pohl if he knew of anybody who might like to publish one. He sent me to Alex Hillman of Hillman Periodicals, who hired me at $85 a week.

The magazine, *Worlds Beyond,* lasted three issues; when Hillman saw the sales reports on the first one, he killed it.

I went back to writing, and sold five or six stories to Horace Gold for *Galaxy.* Ideas came easily, and I was writing the stories as fast as I could type them. Taking this for a permanent condition, I concluded that I didn't have to live in New York if I didn't want to; in 1952 Helen and I sold our furniture, packed up books, typewriters, and cats, and moved to sunny California.

We lived first in a place called La Sierra, a suburb of an only slightly larger place called Riverside, about forty miles from Los Angeles. We bought a car and got in to L.A. once in a while, but didn't have enough money to do it often, and we were beginning to feel isolated. We moved in to Santa Monica, where we rented a tiny one-room apartment over a garage. By this time my sales were drying up and my inspiration too, and I went to work for six weeks in an aircraft plant. When I was laid off there, we decided to go back east.

I knew that Cyril and Mary Kornbluth had gone to upstate New York in search of cheap housing, and we decided to try something like that, only a little closer to New York City. On a map we found interesting place names—Canadensis, Dingmans Ferry—and went out there on a bus. We rented a little house in the woods near Canadensis and I began to write again, but now Horace wasn't buying what I wrote. I turned to book reviews, and did little else for nine years.

In Milford, about twenty miles away, Jim and Virginia Blish had bought a brookside house several years earlier, and we saw them often. Then Judy Merril had come to Milford, rented an old house and brought her two children, Merril and Ann, to live with her. (This eventually led to a messy custody suit.)

Helen and I wanted a larger house and couldn't find one

in Canadensis; Judy, with her usual energy, scoured Milford until she found us a house to rent, and we moved in 1955.

In that year Cyril called me and invited himself down to Milford, where in effect he offered me his friendship—a startling thing to me, because the last time I had seen him, twelve years earlier, he had unscrewed the top of a standing ashtray, spilling butts and ashes on the floor, and then threatened to take my typewriter and hock it for booze money. Pohl was with him, both of them drunk; this may have been the same evening when they set out to kill Lowndes.

In 1956 Judy and I organized the first Milford Science Fiction Writers' Conference, with Jim Blish's nominal help (he was then living in New York, and couldn't participate much). We held it immediately after the science fiction convention in New York, and got forty people, including Theodore Sturgeon, Anthony Boucher, Phil Klass, Robert Silverberg, Harlan Ellison, L. Sprague de Camp, and Forrest J Ackerman. Crammed into the living room of a small tourist cottage on the Delaware, we discussed our topics with an intensity we never achieved again. It was the first such gathering any of us had ever attended, and there was a kind of intoxication in the air.

Cyril had come down from Waverly, New York, bringing with him Jane Roberts, a young writer who lived in nearby Erie. Jane was slender and dark, thin to the point of emaciation; she had enormous dark eyes.

Toward the middle of the week, Cyril invited Blish, Algis Budrys and me to a meeting in Jane's hotel room late at night. With himself and Jane, that made five of us. Cyril had a bottle or two and offered us drinks; he told us that he had wanted to get us together because he thought we were the most important writers there. Looking back, I see this explanation as inadequate—why not Sturgeon, for instance?

I have often wished I had asked Cyril what he really had in mind and what he expected to happen. My memories of what did happen are fragmentary. I remember that after a while Jane was sitting on a straight chair with the rest of us grouped around her, and that she went into a trance and prophesied. I have forgotten every word of what she said. Still later we were grouped in a tight circle with our arms around each other; all the lights had been turned out except one dim one; it may have been a candle. Cyril was expressing his misery, and I began to sob, feeling as I did so that I was crying as his surrogate. We left the meeting with a feeling of closeness that went beyond friendship.

The next day and the next it was still on us, and we drove around town, not going anywhere, just wanting to be together. After the Conference we corresponded for a while in a round-robin letter, and I remember that Cyril said, "I feel I've just acquired a bunch of brothers and sisters."

It seemed to me that there was more to it than that—that we made up a unity of some kind, composed of two pairs—Cyril the dark analog of Budrys, I the blond analog of Blish—around the central figure of Jane.

I know that Cyril was interested in witchcraft and knowledgeable about it, and I know he knew Jane was capable of going into spontaneous trance. I don't think what happened to us was an accident; I think he planned it, but how much he foresaw of what happened I don't know.

After a while the group dissolved, partly due to my feeling that Jane did not contribute to the group feeling when we were not assembled—she was a catalyst or focus of some kind when we were together, but that didn't work by correspondence. But the affection the rest of us felt for each other remained undiminished for years.

Budrys wrote me in 1976, "What we had, I'm sure, was a feedback high. One that compares strongly to the Five experience was the time an engineer, a product manager, and I brought two experimental motor homes from Tulsa to Fort Wayne through a series of mechanical, environmental and personal disasters, trying to maintain a delivery schedule despite blowouts, loose wheels, electrical failures, sensory deprivation through enclosure in air-conditioned humming boxes on superhighways for ten- to twelve-hour periods, broken steering arms, a wrenched back, high fog, and finally a tornado, at whose height we dragged two kids out of the back of an overturned pickup truck. For seventy-two hours, Frank, Rod and I were the only three inhabitants of a mobile pocket universe, sharing a single purpose, communicating only with each other and with rapidly decreasing need for words because we were expressing common concepts with gestures, and encountering increasing difficulty in relating to the outside world at all. We were, by the end of it, almost telepathic, intensely superstitious, on the verge of tears, and so wedded to one another that Frank apologized to me for having to go home to his wife. I have rarely been so proud of myself as a human being, or so aware of the strictures and limitations imposed by the conventions of ordinary human existence."

Waverly, New York, according to Budrys, is "a one-street town made up as a red-brick false-front gulch, bleached, dusty, composed entirely of hardware stores and populated by eunuchoid men in darned railroad overalls, with outlying farms. Cyril's farmhouse had no running water, and a tainted well. A neighbor had a good well, two 1920s Rolls Royces going to hell in the front yard, and was a glass sculptor."

After the Conference, Budrys drove Jane and Cyril home—first Erie, then Waverly. "Cyril had offered to put me up for the night before I turned back to Red Bank. (It's a lot of miles round trip, and I was bushed from Milford and the Nycon.) But Mary made him kick me out; they hadn't seen each other in weeks, and their reunion was tearful and passionate, so I turned around and went home. I don't blame them. I remember drifting through Milford in the middle of the night, dead asleep with a hundred miles to go, but I don't remember what I was thinking."

The Milford Conference became an annual event, and the same thing happened that had happened repeatedly in the Futurian Society—tension developed between the two strongest personalities, in this case Judy and me. Judy has an enviable talent for extempore public speaking; she can go on indefinitely if nobody stops her, and it became more and more difficult to stop her.

With occasional transgressions, we had established the principle that no one who was not a professional science fiction writer should sit in on our afternoon workshop sessions. (Spouses of writers were allowed to attend the evening sessions, but they were expected to be seen and not heard.) There were several challenges to this principle; one year Virginia wanted to be admitted as Jim's collaborator, and I made them both angry by refusing. Another year Judy wanted her daughter Merril to attend, and still another year her third husband, Danny Sugrue, did attend, and wanted to talk. Still another year, Judy proposed a sweeping reorganization under which the s.f. requirement would be dropped and anybody who wanted to attend would be allowed to. She told us that she would resign as a sponsor of the Conference if the vote on this question went against her, and it did. I took over the whole management of the Conference, ran all the sessions, and felt hard-hearted but victorious.

With the exception of *Analog,* which has been profitable for years, science fiction magazines have always been uncertain money-makers. They survived (but just barely) the Depression, the collapse of the pulp industry in the early fifties, the advent of television, the ballooning costs of the seventies. No publisher except Gernsback has ever taken these magazines very seriously, and their combined circulation has apparently stabilized at about 300,000.

In such a feeble industry, it may seem curious that so many writers have become rich and famous. The explanation is that since 1950 science fiction writers have not been entirely dependent on the magazines. Until that date, with rare exceptions, s.f. novels were published only as magazine serials. Since then, in both hard covers and paperback, s.f. novels have been published in annually increasing numbers. This has meant prosperity for many writers who have capitalized on work done before 1950, and for others to whom the magazines were never a primary market.

Why science fiction should have taken so long to become a commercial genre in book publishing, or why it should have taken still longer to penetrate the visual media, I don't know. What I *think* is that it took twenty-five years for the teen-age readers of Gernsback's magazines to grow up and take over positions of influence in schools and libraries, and then another twenty-five years for the teen-agers who went to those schools and borrowed books from those libraries to grow up and assume positions of influence, etc.

The commercial history of science fiction seems to me to have been governed by three factors: the strong appeal of science fiction to young people; the extreme conservatism of the literary establishment; and the decline of magazine fiction since 1940. The establishment's conservatism has been overcome gradually over the last fifty years, producing a rising curve in book publication; but in magazines this is canceled out by the descending curve of *all* magazine fiction, and the result is that the s.f. magazines are barely holding their own.

I confess that I exaggerated a little in chapter six when I compared sex and beauty unfavorably to the thrill of reading science fiction. But the fascination of the unknown, along with sex and beauty, is one of the most powerful human obsessions. Science fiction exploits this fascination, which readily attaches itself to messianic or utopian impulses; in a sense, the Marxists of Europe and Asia are living in a science fiction world, and so are Donald A. Wollheim and Isaac Asimov, who, if I understand what they say, truly believe that humanity has a mighty mission to colonize the planets of other stars.

Virginia Kidd told me, "Jim used to drink three quarts of beer a day when I first met him, which had gone up to four quarts a day shortly after, and he drank a slowly increasing number of quarts of beer per night, every night, for almost as long as I knew him. I used to order beer by the case, and he was up to eight and nine quarts when we separated. He claimed that he worked it off—he used it as fuel—but it was clearly visible in his manuscripts, which used to run along for five or six pages just about error-free. On the sixth or seventh page there would begin to be rather heavy mistakes, and by the eighth, if he went on to the eighth, it was almost unreadable. And at that point he would stop working and start listening to music, and then would slowly become blotto as the evening progressed, from about one o'clock until four or five or six."

When I first knew Jim, the beer he drank never seemed to affect him in any way, but when we met again in Milford he had switched to martinis and after one or two was visibly zonked.

I remember one evening I picked up some piece of furniture that Virginia wanted moved, and Jim was indignant that I was strong enough to lift it. "You used to be weak like me!" he said.

"He's weak, but he's nasty," said Virginia with a grin.

In 1955 the Delaware and the Sawkill flooded the Blishes' house; there was four feet of water in the living room. The place was uninhabitable, and they had to leave Milford. They moved to Brooklyn, then took an apartment on West 84th Street in Manhattan.

Kidd said, "Both in Brooklyn and on 84th Street, Cyril spent a lot of time with us. He would come over from Levittown, and we went out—I had the car then. They visited us and we visited them—they brought the two kids, and it was really horrible. John would run the length of our eight-room apartment screaming—howling. And Mary would be quietly trying to keep him quiet and out of Cyril's hair. Cyril would get paler and paler. I remember once we went out there at Christmas time—we made a special trip because Jim had money to give Cyril for his story in the first issue of *Vanguard—the* issue of *Vanguard**—and Mary was painting a great bare branch that had fallen off a tree. That was their Christmas tree; she was

---

* *Vanguard Science Fiction,* edited by Blish. It was killed off even faster than my *Worlds Beyond.*

painting it orange, I think, or painting it some other color to go up against an orange backdrop. It was like a big piece of driftwood with bare branches on which she was going to hang Christmas-tree balls. And they had been planning to get through Christmas with no money at all, quietly starving.

"But whenever we were together with them and the kids, it was incredibly stressful. John wanted so badly to communicate, and was so totally unable to, that he couldn't allow people to communicate in his presence—he always made sufficient noise so that there was just no chance. And it was awful to see Mary trying to cope. There were a very few occasions—I don't remember how it happened, probably Cyril took the boys out for ten minutes or something like that—that Mary and I had a chance to sit and talk for a couple of minutes. She was marvelous. I liked her. But I didn't get a chance to know her the way I did Cyril.

"When he used to arrive in Brooklyn, he would be wearing a homburg and carrying a rolled umbrella—he looked like a Jewish accountant. We lived in an area of Hasidim, and he looked like any one of those guys coming home, who would expect his wife to have the table ready, and go sit down and eat his supper. Those were his go-to-New-York-and-see-people clothes, I think.

"And one of the first things he would do would be to take a shower, and I seem to remember him running barefoot up and down the hall—that was also a very long apartment—and sort of squealing with joy.

"And he was open, and sensitive, and—you know, *there*. Every bit of him was there, and attentive, and forthcoming. When Cyril was there, Jim would put aside whatever his routine was and the three of us would talk; or if Jim wasn't there yet, Cyril and I would talk, and we'd talk as if we had been shot out from slingshots—*wham,* and start talking. And I think it was important to Cyril, I think it was how he got through the Levittown period, or at least part of it. And it was important to me.

"And I remember specifically, after the first Milford where the love feast occurred—when the Five were formed—Cyril came to me to talk about it. And Ben was at a particularly unloveable stage of his infancy at that point; he cried an awful lot—he had been sick a good deal. I picked him up to stop his crying and walked with him—and Cyril and I paced up and down our living room with Ben howling on my arm, and Cyril and I talking earnestly over this howling. Finally in sheer despair I put Ben down, and immediately he stopped crying.

"But the gist of our conversation was—I passionately wanted in, not as Jim's wife, not *because* I was Jim's wife, but because they were five people all of whom—four of whom—I knew and loved and felt I could interact with. And Cyril, I think, was more actively feeling that no wife should be in *because* she was a wife. And I think he felt and said that more strongly when he was not in my presence. In my presence he said that of course I belonged in, and that he personally would like to have me in, and nonetheless it was the Five, and as soon as somebody else was in, it would be a Six, it wouldn't be the same group. And I was aware even before we started talking that this was so, and it was a hopeless kind of thing to want to be part of it, and yet I wanted passionately to be in it because it was the first interesting thing that had happened in a long time, intellectually.

"None of the Five would discuss it, it was a closed subject. I think Jane was a focus . . . but everybody was a clam. Nobody would talk about what had happened. And I think now very much, at a remove of very many years, that nobody really knew what had happened. I got the feeling that everybody thought

Cyril was the leader, and Jane was the witch—that he was using Jane's potential to bind you all into something that had never happened before. It was maybe something on the order of *More Than Human.**

"Cyril told me that he knew he was cruel—and I told him I knew he wasn't, and he said, 'You don't know, you don't know. There are hidden things about me, I am a cruel person.' This was while we were walking up and down the living room. And I figured what he was talking about was the trunk full of strange lingerie and what-nots that I had heard about. All I know is that he got Mary to dress up in strange outfits ever so often—he was a lingerie freak, and so was Jim."

I asked her, "You mean like merry widows?"

"Probably—that was about Jim's taste. And they were kept in a locked trunk—these special accouterments, for evenings of wild passion, once they'd finally gotten those kids to sleep. But I know I assumed that was what he meant—that he was cruel to Mary—he felt he was cruel to Mary, that he left her cooped up with the kids while he went off, because he couldn't stand it. He would fling out of their house in Levittown and just walk because he couldn't stand it. And Mary couldn't go out and walk if she couldn't stand it, because there was nobody to stay with the kids.

"But I now think what he actually meant was that he was going to be cruel enough to keep me out, no matter how much I wanted in."

Pohl said, "Cyril and I were sitting around drinking and talking, and we were talking about ways we wished we were dif-

---

*Theodore Sturgeon's novel about a group personality.

ferent, and Cyril said, 'The only thing I can wish for myself is that I were less cruel.'

"I went up to see him in Levittown once, and there was a big picture Johnny Michel had painted on the wall, all amorphous black and red, and Cyril was giving me an interpretation of it: 'This is the triumph of the Id over the Superego, and this big black smear is Death and Devastation as Perfuckpersonified by Daddy.'

"Cyril was a difficult, obstinate, temperamental sort of person, and I would not be surprised if he had the same opinion of me. And there were times when over some grievance or other we just wouldn't be speaking for a while. After he moved to Long Island, we went through a couple times of not speaking very much, which is one reason why we only wrote the novels we did together.

"The last prolonged contact I had with Cyril was about a year before he died or a little less, when he had come out to talk and we had chatted awhile. We had just written *Wolfbane,* a short version of it. And he reported that he was in bad trouble on a novel called *The Crater,* which was about the Civil War. And I said, 'Well, you want to collaborate on it?' and he said yeah.

"So he sent me the manuscript and I read it and wrote back what I thought it needed, and he wrote back saying, 'Fine, now that you've told me what I needed to know, send back the manuscript, I don't need you to collaborate.' Pissed me off. He never finished it."

I told him, "Somebody said that it was almost as if Cyril knew he was going to die young."

"Oh, he knew. He was told that he had essential malignant hypertension, acquired from carrying a fifty-caliber machine gun around the Battle of the Bulge, in below-zero weather, forty hours at a stretch. A circulatory thing, where your heart just cannot push blood fast enough. Anyhow, it's hypertension because the heart's under strain all the time. So the doctor said, 'You can take this stuff I will give you,' which was a rauwolfia derivative, 'and in future you must never again taste salt or smoke a cigarette, or consume alcohol. And if you do any of these things you'll die within a year.'

"Cyril tried it for about a month, and he was not the same person. Cyril was about the quickest person I've ever known. He didn't know everything, but he knew a lot, and he knew what he didn't know. He didn't ever think he knew something that he didn't really know. But while he was here that time, he was incoherent and bumbling and couldn't remember things. I think he decided he didn't want to live that way. So he went back to all his bad habits, and like the doctor said, he died within a year."

Kornbluth had a heart attack in the winter of 1958. He had been offered the job of editing *Fantasy & Science Fiction,* and was on his way into town to talk to the publisher. He shoveled out his driveway, drove to the station, and collapsed; he died without regaining consciousness two hours later. He was thirty-four.

Several Futurians saw John Michel occasionally during the fifties. Fred Pohl remembered meeting him at a convention; he said Michel was "obese and flabby." Shaw told me that Michel used to drop in to see him every now and then, and that he was apparently in abject poverty. "Johnny's eyes were bad, and he had constructed a pair of eyeglasses for himself out of old lenses and wire. And he was making table decorations out of colored glass and metal, trying to peddle them, and I believe twice I loaned him ten bucks, and he promised someday to give me one of these table decorations, or as many of them as I could use."

Wollheim told me, "A guy who used to write for me at Ace Books knew Johnny slightly. He said he met him on the street, and Johnny asked to borrow ten bucks. He said, 'I gave it to him, because I figured I'd never see him again if I did, and it was worth it.' "

I knew from Wollheim that Michel had been living in Greenwood Lake, New York, and that he had died in 1968, but my letter addressed to his estate there came back stamped "unforwardable." Wollheim had broken with Michel years before: his information came from an official of the Smithsonian Institution, with whom Michel had had some correspondence. I wrote to the Smithsonian, but they could tell me nothing more.

I let months go by while I tried to think of some way of locating Michel's widow. Finally I did what I should have thought of doing in the first place: I called the postmaster in Greenwood Lake. He had known both the Michels; he told me they had moved years ago to Middletown, New York, and that Joan had worked on the newspaper there. Middletown is not more than thirty miles from Milford, Pennsylvania, where I had been living at the time.

I found Joan Michel and her fourteen-year-old son Hilary in a comfortably cluttered garret apartment, and we sat at her kitchen table talking about John. She is a tall, big-boned, deep-bosomed woman, not pretty or even handsome, but when she smiles her face lights up with amusement, affection, self-mockery. Her voice is extraordinarily clear and musical. Some of the things she said about her life with Michel sound bitter in print, but she spoke them without complaint, in a lyrical, wistful tone. When she said, "And he *left me,* with no *money,*" the emphasized words went up in pitch rather than down.

Joan Michel's father, James Joseph Martin, was Irish, her mother Jewish. They were separated before Joan was born. She lived with her mother, an unemployed garment worker, until she was twenty months old, then with a foster mother in Groton, Connecticut, until she was ten, when her mother took her back.

At summer camp, when she was seventeen, she met a

young man and was attracted to him, but he went into the army in the following year. Joan attended Boston University, then transferred to the University of North Carolina in Chapel Hill; she graduated with a B.A. in drama in 1945. She met her friend from summer camp when he got out of the army in 1946 and they were married. Their son Gregory was born on Christmas Day, 1947; she never saw the father again after she became pregnant. Gregory, born partially blind and with cerebral palsy, was two and a half when she met John Michel in March 1950, at a benefit movie performance for a leftist cause.

"There was this guy across the room, wearing a checked flannel shirt with orange in it, sketching something on the wall, and a little something in my head said, 'Joan, whatever you do, have nothing to do with *that* particular man.' He came over afterward, and asked me out for a cup of coffee, and was telling me how he had been married before, but he was very jealous, and that had destroyed the marriage, but he saw the error of his ways and wouldn't make that mistake again."

Joan is convinced that it was the knowledge that she had already had a child that made Michel determined to marry her. He had recently been divorced from the second of two wives, both of whom had turned out to be barren. Michel had had his sperm tested, and knew the fault was not his. In his journal he wrote that the first wife, Annie, "wore yards of toilet chain as necklaces and bracelets, and bathed in perfume but not often in water." Abbie, the second, became a fiercer Red than Michel after their marriage, and once accused him of cowardice when he left a picket line, to which he had been assigned by the Party, because he was afraid of being beaten up by waterfront goons—any physical injury could have made his osteo flare up again.

For this and other reasons, Michel's relationship with the Party had been unsatisfactory for some time. His attendance at meetings had been spotty; he had been given several consecutive leaves of absence. Finally, in late 1949, the Party gently suggested that he drop out, and he did so.

In the summer of 1949, after his separation from Abbie, Michel had gone to live in an unheated cottage he and the Wollheims had bought together a year earlier, in Bloomington, New York, near Kingston. He was out of a job, supporting himself by free-lance comics writing. What he wanted to do was to write a serious novel. "My record to date," he wrote in his journal, "is three articles, one of them on the atom bomb, for the *New Masses,* book reviews for the *New Masses,* and four short stories for the Sunday edition of the *Worker.* Not a miserly contribution to my political creed, but not enough. For now and for some time past I have wished to put down what I know is in me in a novel, a great novel of myself, my friends, my enemies and my own times. . . . Perhaps my magnum opus (it will be the first of about three, I think) will now be written."

Meanwhile the electricity was off, there was nothing to eat in the house, it was raining, and "my dearest friends, Elsie and Donald Wollheim, had thoughtfully removed the electric water heater on their last trip here."

In the fall, with nothing written, he went back to New York. In March he met Joan, and in April they were married.

They spent their honeymoon in the Bloomington cottage, where Joan cooked on a kerosene stove, and John wrote two comics continuities to meet deadlines. He began work on his novel, *God's Roost,* a roman à clef about the Ivory Tower. He eventually wrote about thirty thousand words of the novel; it is disappointing as fiction, but contains recognizable portraits of most of the Futurians.

Michel's marital troubles had put a strain on his friendship with the Wollheims. He had quarreled violently with Annie when he discovered she could not conceive.

"It got to be an unbearable situation," Wollheim told me. "We were always in the position where his wife would come around to our house at night crying, and we'd have to commiserate with her, and then finally Anne broke with him. The next thing we knew, he took up with Anne's friend, Abbie, who was a dancing instructor and a professional modern dancer. She was a big, gawky, good-looking gal, with a very sweet heart. And he did the same thing with her, after a few months—she didn't get pregnant, so he began to accuse her of meeting people on the stairs of the house—they were living on West 4th Street—and he would throw things, and she would come around to our house crying, and we'd spend a few hours patting her brow."

Elsie put in: "And then Johnny came around and he and Donald had a *fist fight.*"

"He accused me of sleeping with her," Wollheim said, "and we had a terrific battle. Then the next day he came out all remorseful and that sort of thing."

They patched it up and remained on friendly terms, but the old intimacy was gone. Michel noted in his journal early in 1949 that he seldom saw "the Wollies" now and had little to say to them. In December he wrote:

Lines composed while waiting for Elsie and Donald Wollheim to show up (which they didn't) for an appointment at the Museum of Modern Art:

In goldenrod and plaster wet,
In scrape from off a belly sore,
In salesman's throat unchoked as yet
In underwear of some old whore . . .
Let D. and E. be fricasseed and fried!
In crawling soup a year since spoiled,

In Truman's guts and undistilled,
In blood of toads, but served up mulled,
In bourgeoisie a month since killed . . .
Let D. and E. be fricasseed and fried!
In lipstick kissed away from apes,
In greenish night-soil heaped and spread,
In vinegar that once was grapes,
In roaches' juice—and they not dead . . .
Let D. and E. be fricasseed and fried!

John and Joan went to live in a housing development in Long Island City. He legally adopted her son Gregory, and at his insistence she became pregnant again almost immediately.

Wollheim and Michel quarreled again in 1950. Wollheim needed an assistant editor at Avon, and offered Michel the job. Michel first accepted, then refused. Wollheim blamed Joan for his change of mind; he had convinced himself that she was a "welfare moocher" who would lose her benefits if Michel took a job. "And at that point I said, 'The hell with you, fella, I mean this is it, I've had it up to here.' "

Joan Michel bore twins, Shawn and Kate, on December 29, 1950. Kate died at eight weeks, fighting for breath in her father's arms, in the ambulance on the way to the hospital.

That winter John and Joan decided to leave the housing development, where they had had problems with vandalism and theft; Michel said he wanted to get out of the city altogether, away from everyone he knew. He drove out to the Poconos, went through Milford without attempting to see the Blishes, although he knew they were living there, and found a house for rent in Greenwood Lake, a small rural community about twenty-five miles from Port Jervis, New York, just across the state line from Milford. They moved in February. From the beginning things went badly.

Michel's income from comic-strip writing was gone; both he and Joan were trying to support themselves by other kinds of free-lance writing in which neither had much experience. They wrote confession stories and popular medical articles; Michel designed a series of tin-can motors and sold *Popular Science* several articles about them, later collected into a children's book, *Small Motors You Can Make* (Van Nostrand, 1963). They were desperately poor; because Shawn was still an infant, Joan could not get a job, and John would not. Instead, he spent his time making lamps from his own designs out of sheet metal, stained glass and other materials. One of them was a wooden box with rods of Lucite projecting in all directions; he offered it to Lightolier, and it aroused some interest, but the company turned it down in the end as too hard to manufacture.

By the early fifties Michel's appearance and behavior had changed radically. Although he was not dropsical, as Pohl thought, he had gained so much weight that he was almost unrecognizable; he had also grown a scraggly goatee. His compulsive neatness was gone; he was slovenly in his dress, not scrupulously clean, and sometimes even neglected to brush his teeth.

The fact that he never tried to get in touch with his former friends in Milford seems to confirm Wollheim's account of the break with Blish, Lowndes, Merril and Kidd. We have already seen that he chose his sexual partners on political grounds. His journals reveal that he consulted psychoanalysts several times during the forties, and that he chose them the same way. In his journal he complains about one of them that after telling Michel he could say anything he liked, the analyst refused to let him talk about politics.

Michel kept up a correspondence with a few Party friends, and with the editors of the *Worker* and the *New Masses*; he made two or three friends in Greenwood Lake, including a teen-aged boy whom he adopted as a protégé, and to whom he wrote embarrassing fake-pontifical letters; but he often complained that he had no intellectual companionship. Having cut himself off from all the Futurians except the Wollheims, and having dropped out of the Party by request, Michel had lost nearly all the friends he had. Then he lost the Wollheims too. A dispute over the sale of the house they owned together led to coolness, then to outright hostility. Michel stopped seeing the Wollheims, and his comments about them in his journals thereafter were few and bitter.

Michel was being driven by forces he did not understand and could not control. His attitude toward women was a paradoxical combination of worship and contempt. He idolized motherhood and looked to his wife for security, but he wrote to a friend, Robert Schuman, in the fifties: "You want to get the facts straight on women, Bob? Read an article titled 'The Natural Inferiority of Women' in the latest issue of *Bluebook*. . . . The point is that it has now been proven that a woman simply cannot deal with complicated reasoning as efficiently as a man, and there's no point in trying to make them as efficient in this department. The only solution is love and the rod and patience. Or a good backhand crack across the cheek will do, provided it is delivered in hot anger. . . ."

Like many writers, he had conflicting superiority and inferiority feelings. He wanted to be a serious writer, or perhaps a poet, but a nagging self-doubt kept him from trying hard enough to put his ability to the test. His Catholic upbringing, which he never entirely forsook, had transferred itself in his mind to his Communist faith. As Joan put it, "He simply took all the rigidities of Catholicism, the hierarchical system and the 'being saved,' you know, and the Day of Judgment and all that, and transferred it to Communism."

Michel was careful to keep a copy of everything he wrote, and often expressed the hope that his writings would be preserved after his death; he was tormented by the thought that Joan might throw them away. He made a large wooden box, about the size of a cedar chest, filled it with his manuscripts, letters and journals, and secured it with a padlock.

His journals, which he kept from 1948 to 1952 and from 1955 to 1960, are full of rambling political diatribes. He was convinced that he was in danger of persecution because of his politics. In the late forties he sent several stories to John Campbell, the editor of *Astounding Science Fiction,* and got them back with curt rejection notes. Then he tried one under a pseudonym, got a more cordial letter, and concluded that he was on a blacklist. He was sure he was being constantly watched by the FBI. "Aw, come on, you're small potatoes," Joan said to him. "No, I'm not, I'm very *important,"* he answered.

In fact, he may have been interviewed by the FBI in the late fifties. Wollheim told me, "After we'd broken with Michel, two FBI men came up to my office. Mostly they were asking about William Sykora, oddly enough, who must have had a very weird record. If you study Sykora's history, you'll find there was a brief period when he was issuing Communistic statements. And I don't know whether that was a phony, whether it was a put-on, what he was trying to do, but apparently the FBI became very interested in him since he was also apparently involved in rocketry later on, or they had heard of his early experiments.

"And they swung around to asking questions about other people, and they asked two or three questions which could only have come from Johnny Michel. They said certain things and mentioned certain names which nobody could have known except Michel. I denied anything about it, I didn't know what they were talking about. But I was convinced that it was Michel, because for one reason, he never communicated with me ever again."

In 1953 Michel's mother's last surviving sister died and left him ten thousand dollars, about a third of it in AT & T stock. Joan wanted to keep the stock, but Michel said, "I don't believe in the capitalist system, I'm not going to do one thing to support it." They sold the stock for three thousand dollars.

They used the money to buy two acres in Pleasant Valley, near Poughkeepsie, and build a prefab house. Their mortgage payments were forty-seven dollars a month. Joan said, "That I will never forget, because we went to the closing at the bank, and I had to excuse myself and go to the ladies' room, and when I came back the bankers were in a state of dismay, because while I was gone John took the opportunity to say he didn't think he wanted to go through with it after all—forty-seven dollars a month was too much to pay."

Throughout the years of their marriage Michel had been drinking almost continually. Beer and wine were his tipples. A gallon jug of wine usually lasted him two days. He had always been abusive when he was drunk, and now he became incoherent. One day, when Joan nagged him to get a job, he flew into a rage and began throwing furniture. Joan was frightened and asked a neighbor to call the state police. When the troopers came, they told her that if she pressed charges, Michel would have to go either to jail or to a mental hospital. She chose the hospital, and had him committed to the Hudson River Psychiatric Center, where he underwent shock treatments in August 1956.

When he came back, Joan said, "He was quite a different person, he was very relaxed, at ease, very pleasant to be with, very interested in the children, but that wore off." In September, he applied for a job as feature editor on the Poughkeepsie *New Yorker* ("a sweatshop of a newspaper," Michel said) and got it.

"It was the only job he ever held in all the years we were married. He made it his business to come in fifteen minutes, twenty minutes late. He said, 'When you have a job, never come on time—let them know you're independent.' He'd take a bottle to the office and stick it in his desk, and he'd come back and say, 'See, you're forcing me to work, and you're forcing me to drink, because I can't stand working and you're driving me to drink.' "

Late in 1957 Michel suggested moving away from Poughkeepsie. "He was always afraid that as long as we were there, I might do something like that again." (Put him in the hospital.) He wanted to go to California. Joan told him they could sell the house and take a trip to California, or buy another place in Greenwood Lake, but probably not both; he chose California.

They settled in Hayward, near San Francisco. Michel was working on a young people's book about famous battles for which he had a contract with Bobbs-Merrill. (Later the publishers sent him a critical report based on the comments of teen-agers to whom they had shown the manuscript, and Michel was so infuriated that he refused to make any changes; the book was never published.)

Michel was getting unemployment compensation, but it was not enough. Joan took a job packing boxes for Montgomery Ward, then became a secretary for General Electric. Then Michel said he couldn't stand California and wanted to go back east. They returned to Greenwood Lake in the summer of 1958.

Joan took a job as legal secretary with a firm in Warwick. Michel interested himself in civic affairs, painted signs for the library, made suggestions about beautifying the village. In 1960 he proposed that the village put up a monument commemorating a mail-carrying rocket flight launched from Greenwood Lake in 1936 by a group led by Willy Ley, five months after Will Sykora's Long Island experiment. Ley built two liquid-fuel rockets, the *Gloria I* and *Gloria II*, and loaded them with letters bearing special commemorative stamps. *Gloria I* skidded across the frozen lake for only a hundred and twenty-five yards, but *Gloria II* soared a full three hundred yards and crashed on the New Jersey shore.

The monument was erected in front of the Greenwood Lake library and dedicated on February 23, 1961, the twenty-fifth anniversary of the flight. As a result of his efforts, Michel was elected an honorary member of the local chamber of commerce, and faithfully attended its meetings thereafter, gorging himself on canapes.

Joan was pregnant again in the fall of 1960. "In October or November of that year, Scott Meredith, who had been John's agent on and off for all these years—John always called him Feebleman—called and said he'd gotten a deal where he had to supply forty-eight or fifty novels in a short time, and he asked John if he would like to do some." They were porn novels, for Beacon Books. "So I said, 'This is great, just when we need it, because I'll be having to quit my job.' "

They agreed that they would both write novels for Beacon and would work out the plots together. "When I met John, I was going to be a serious writer, and I had done some critical works and so on—didn't know anything about commercial writing. John taught me all that. But his mind was not as fertile as mine. So he and I would sit down and talk together. I'd say, 'I see this happening, and that,' and we'd go along, and he'd very sardonically nod, and then he'd say, 'Well, that's wrong,' and we'd work out the plots, for both his novels and mine, and sit down and write them."

Michel wrote four novels for Beacon, all under the

James Blish (photo by Jay Kay Klein).

Above left, Joan and John Michel, 1950. *Top right,* Michel, 1960. *Opposite top,* Isaac Asimov, 1971 (photo by Jay Kay Klein). *Opposite bottom,* Richard Wilson, 1975 (photo by Damon Knight).

Top, Judith Merril, 1970 (photo by Jay Kay Klein). *Above,* Donald A. Wollheim, 1975 (photo by Damon Knight). *Opposite,* Robert A.W. Lowndes, 1975 (photo by Damon Knight).

Frederik Pohl, 1975.

pseudonym "Louis Richard": *The Sex Pulse,* 1961; *And Sex Is the Payoff* and *Secret Lusts,* 1962; *Artist's Woman,* 1963. They are commercial fiction of a high order of competence, better written than most science fiction, and much better than Michel's "serious" novel, *God's Roost.*

All four of the novels are juvenile and neurotic in their attitude toward women, but they are well organized and at times eloquent, even lyrical. Here is a sentence from *The Sex Pulse,* page 155: (The hero is embracing a girl in the twilight.) "His body seemed to melt into hers as though they were two chocolate creams being crushed together in the magic mouth of the night." And another, from page 156: "She smoothed her dress and took his hand, and he followed her, drunk with that revelation of sweetness and conquest that is part of puppy love and first love, and which is the best and most glorious of all the treasures of man's consciousness."

It seems to me now that he really deeply felt certain rather shallow things. And maybe that was the tragedy of Michel, that all his depth was in shallow places.

Michel was sentimental about his children, but unpredictable and sometimes cruel to them. "Once when I was pregnant with Hilary, and he was beating Shawn before going to school," Joan told me, "I said, 'That's it—the next time you beat one of my kids I'll take a strap or a dog leash and I will beat you.' And I said, 'I'm pregnant with this one—don't you ever lay a hand on this one.' And he never did."

Hilary (named after Hilaire Belloc) was born in July 1961. Six months later the Michels had to leave their rented house. "And all the time we were moving he was saying, 'Excuse me, I've got to go to the state hospital, I'm afraid I'm going to commit suicide.' I'd say, 'Could you please wait until we get the unpacking done?' 'No,' he'd say, 'I've got to go now, I'm afraid I'm going to kill myself.' So as soon as we moved into the other place, he just called the doctor and off he went. And left me, with no money."

Michel had another course of shock treatments, followed by outpatient therapy, and again seemed improved for a while. During the next few years Joan talked of separation or divorce, and there were constant quarrels. Michel signed himself into the hospital several more times voluntarily, usually for only a few weeks at a time.

In 1964 Joan got a job as a reporter with the Middletown *Times Herald Record;* it involved a good deal of travel; she often had to work six or seven days a week. "And the boys were still quite little then, except for Gregory. And John was drinking heavily, running around the village cashing checks and drinking—going into a drunken stupor—and the boys were just kind of wandering around on their own. Hilary was only two years old, and the neighbors would tell me that sometimes he would just wander around and take care of himself for hours."

The only time she ever touched Michel's manuscripts, she says, was during this period, and it was one of the few times she ever amused him. "You know, here I was, holding down a job, trying to earn a living, with three little kids to take care of, our oldest being severely handicapped, and this guy not lifting a finger to work. I went into a rage, and picked up the stuff he was working on, and threw open the rear door, and I said, 'The trouble with you is you care more about your writings than you do about me.' And I flung them out the door, and I said, 'And that one goes *there,* and that one goes *there'*—flung them all over, and I thought he would be furious. He was amused. He said, *'By God,* I didn't know you had it in you.' "

Michel was working intermittently on a book about boat

models for which he had a contract; he left it with one chapter unwritten. In May 1964 he wrote to a Dr. Katz, at the Orange County Mental Health Clinic in Goshen, "For two years or more, since I have [sic] my original breakdown, I have lost my capacity to write. . . . I went through a terrible period, with my wife castigating me continually in front of the children for not trying to write."

Throughout that summer he sent long letters to local tradespeople complaining of snubs. He suspected the villagers of anti-Semitism, although they had no way of knowing he and Joan were half-Jewish. In June he wrote to the County National Bank to complain of surly responses when he phoned (four times in two weeks) to ask how late the bank was open.

In 1966 the Michels moved to Middletown to cut down on Joan's commuting, and Joan joined the Otisville-Mount Hope Presbyterian Church. Michel would not join, but he sometimes attended services, and became friendly with the pastor, Ronald James. A friend of James's, an ex-minister, owned Jubilee Ranch, a summer resort in nearby Godeffroy, and Michel spent several summers there as arts and crafts counselor. Shawn spent some time there too, and worked at weekend retreats.

In the fall of 1968 Michel was serving as caretaker of Jubilee Ranch, living in a little cabin near the entrance of the property and spending part of his time at home. "He was talking in a chaotic and incoherent way a good part of the time," Joan told me, "so I finally got him certified in the Middletown State Hospital. Then on November 20 he signed himself out and went back to the ranch. There was another old guy living there, and he saw John around for about a day, and then nothing; nobody saw him, nobody heard from him, just disappeared. And I said to Shawn, 'Oh-oh, something's happened.'

"He had about a hundred dollars in his checking account; I thought maybe he'd gone down to the city, but when his statement came back I saw that he'd just cashed one last check, and there was still money in the account. That wasn't like him—he would go through the bank account, to drink—when he got to the bottom of that, he'd keep writing checks. He had cashed a check at a bar on Route 29, and bought a bottle of wine, and that was the last anybody had seen of him.

"On New Year's Day, 1969, about ten o'clock in the morning, I realized John was dead. Shawnie looked at me and said, 'Mom, what's wrong?' And I couldn't tell him, I just knew. I had a vision in my head of Jubilee Ranch, of the front end of it, where John used to live in a little cabin near the stream. And then about eight or nine that night, when we were taking down the Christmas tree, there was a knock on the door and there was a state trooper there, and he said, 'I have something to tell you.' I said, 'I know what it is, you don't have to tell me.'

"The Anderson family used to come up there regularly for weekends, and their youngest son always used to see this thing in the frozen stream; he thought it was just a log there. It was John.

"I called Reverend Jim, and he came to see me. He said John was found drowned in just maybe a foot or a foot and a half of water."

12

Joan Michel, John's widow, is a sturdy, cheerful, self-reliant woman who seems untouched by her long nightmare. Hilary Michel is still at home; he is a bright, friendly fourteen-year-old who likes science fiction and plays the guitar. His older brother Shawn went to Farmington State University College for two years, got his degree in automotive, then went to Pratt for two years on a work-study program. "Since the time he was six," Joan told me, "he's been reading car manuals. I remember when John and I were in California, whatever car we had John always got the manual, and there would be Shawn thumbing through it saying, 'Dad, look, you should saw off the exhaust pipe a little.' And when he was sixteen and lived here, he bought his first car for forty bucks—Christmas money. I thought he was going to take it to bed with him that night. And he's been like that ever since." He lives now in Columbus, Ohio, with his wife, a beautiful Korean woman.

Joan's son Gregory is legally blind; the New York State Commission on the Blind pays for his education as long as he keeps up a certain grade average, and he has been in college since 1968. In the New York University School of Engineering he happened to room with a young Orthodox Jew. In 1972 he became a convert to Hasidic Judaism, and was told by two rabbis that as a Jew he could not have anything to do with Christians. Joan has not seen him since, and can't find out where he is. Although Joan is half Jewish, as John was, Gregory never had any training at home in Judaism. He took to Judaism, she says, as if he had been born to it; she thinks ultimately he will want to settle in Israel. In Brooklyn College he showed a strong interest in Spanish language and culture, took up flamenco guitar, and wrote a thesis on the Sephardic Jews.

In the winter of 1962 the Blishes' marriage broke up; a year later Blish married Judith Ann Lawrence, who has a large, pillowy figure not unlike Virginia's. A talented illustrator, she sat for years on the fringes of the discussions at Milford, and went home every year with a raging desire to write, only to realize, "But I don't *want* to be a writer!" Eventually she gave in, and the last I heard, after Blish's death, she had published a number of stories and had written a novel.

In the early sixties, Blish had been working for a public relations firm with tobacco accounts, and his assignment had been to rebut the evidence for a link between smoking and cancer. In 1963 Blish, a heavy cigarette smoker, was operated on for cancer of the tongue; he told me later that the operation had been performed without anesthetic. (At various times Blish told me other unbelievable things, and I later found out that some of them were not true.)

In 1969 Jim and Judith moved to England, where they

rented a house near Oxford, then bought one which they called "Treetops." Jim was working on a three-volume history of witchcraft commissioned by Doubleday, and on a long technical work about music, neither of which he finished. To meet expenses, he wrote a series of fictionalized versions of *Star Trek* episodes, and for the first time in his life got large quantities of fan mail.

In 1974 he was operated on for lung cancer and made an apparently good recovery, but that did not last; ten months later he died.

Virginia wrote to me, "During the last year of Jim's life, he had an intense autumnal love affair with a younger, attractive, sensitive English fantasy writer. She was good friends with Judy as well. She initially sat at Jim's feet, learning, worshiping (a posture I recognize). The last few weeks of his life she was at Treetops and so was Beth—and Jim needed all three of them—his daughter, his wife, and his lover."

On the day the news of Blish's death reached America, a fan at the Star Trek convention in Philadelphia picked up one of Blish's *Star Trek* books from a dealer's table and asked, "Is this the guy that died?" When the dealer said yes, the fan asked, "Is he going to be doing any more of these?"

In the early fifties Chester Cohen married Laura Goforth, a music teacher from Chattanooga, where her father had been a member of the law firm of Goforth, Kilburn and Robb. They had three children, one of whom they named after me. In the fifties Helen and I saw a great deal of the Cohens; they came up to Milford on weekends, and then bought a little cottage on the Sawkill, where Chester now lives year-round. He has no occupation; he sometimes refinishes furniture as a hobby. In the late forties he had several series of insulin shock treatments for depression, and since then has been on a regimen of tranquilizers.

Sometime in the late sixties Mary Kornbluth drove out to Milford with Manny Mitteman, a manufacturer of sophisticated bugging and anti-bugging devices for organized crime, who bore a striking physical resemblance to Cyril. They brought a bottle of Spanish brandy, and as the evening progressed Mary put most of it away. She wept as she told me about her cancer, and the radiation treatments that had made her body look sunburned. Then she grew hysterical, wailing, "You're going to live, and *I'm not!*" Mittleman gave me an oh-my-God look and took her away.

I assumed that Mary had been attracted to Mittleman because of his resemblance to Cyril, but Pohl told me it was the other way around—Mittleman was attracted to her because she was Cyril's widow, because he wanted to be Cyril. "He told me that he had developed a hero-worship for Cyril. He called Cyril while he was out here in Red Bank, tried to persuade Cyril to collaborate with him on a story. Cyril just shrugged him off. He is a singularly loathsome person. He tells the most rotten stories about himself.

"I can tell you the last time I talked to Mary, come to think of it. Because it was shortly after the last time I saw Manny, and that was October of '71. And Mary called me and said she wanted something, probably money. And I mentioned I'd seen Manny, and she said, 'Under no circumstances are you to let him know where I am.'

"Something turned Gillespie off, and I don't know what," Pohl said. "He wound up running a plastic cooker in Pottstown, Pennsylvania, or something like that, polymerizing long-chain molecules into plastic, last I heard. So far as I know he has not tried to do anything more complex than that in the last twenty-five years.

"I think what happened to Jack was that he got into the merchant marine, and lived in a completely unintellectual and kind of shit-filled environment for three or four years, and couldn't get out of it. He joined the merchant marine in lieu of army service during World War II. What he didn't know, what none of the merchant marine people knew, was that when the war was over and they left the merchant marine, they would all be immediately drafted. So he stayed on in the merchant marine rather than be drafted. He was still shipping out from time to time as late as '51, '52. It wasn't until he married Lois that he gave it up entirely."

After her divorce from Pohl, Doris Baumgardt married Tom Owens, a black-Irish pugilist, poet, artist and writer—"the handsomest man you ever saw in your life," said Rosalind Wylie. After a few years Doris began seeing Dick Wilson. "Finally she just told Tom one day that she was going to leave him and marry Dick. That's when she came to my house with Margot [her year-old daughter by Owens].* And Tom had a nervous breakdown. He wanted to kill Dick."

Rosalind Cohen Wylie was married a second time in 1953 to a businessman, Williams Moore. Wilson and Doris broke up in 1965. She died in 1970 of cancer. Seven months later Moore died of a heart attack.

Wilson, now head of the news bureau of Syracuse University, married Fran Keegan Daniels in 1967; then they got on a

---

*Margot later married Peter Van der Meulen of ABC Radio; they have a son, Dirk, named after Dirk Wylie.

plane and went to the science fiction convention in New York, where Lester del Rey seized the bride, kissed her and said, "This is your lucky day—you got married and met Lester del Rey, all in the same day."

I talked to Judith Merril and Virginia Kidd in my living room in Madeira Beach, Florida; they were both visiting nearby. It was the first time in my five years there that either one had come to Florida: they had dropped into my lap just when I needed them. Judy was restless and a little bored; she showed me how to use my Sony tape recorder, noticed a sticker on the top, and remarked, "They sold you a demo." Several times she turned off the machine when she wanted to say something not for publication. She expressed impatience with the whole idea of talking about the Futurians, but as she warmed to the topic she spoke fluently and to the point.

Both women are matronly; both are in their early fifties. Merril is a successful "documentarist" for CBC Radio in Toronto—she chooses a topic, finds people to talk about it, makes and edits tapes for CBC broadcast. Kidd is a literary agent in Milford, Pennsylvania, where all three of us once lived. Kidd listened as we talked and occasionally chimed in with some recollection or comment of her own. Earlier, in this room, I had taped an interview with her alone; later, on her own initiative, she interviewed Chester Cohen in Milford and sent me the tape.

After her children were grown, in the late fifties, Merril was married once more, to a merchant mariner and union organizer, Daniel Sugrue; they are still married, although they have been separated for thirteen years. In 1966-67 she spent a year in England, where she gathered the material for her "New Wave" anthology, *England Swings SF.*

In 1972 she spent several months in Japan, working with

three Japanese translators on an anthology of Japanese science fiction which is to be published by Bantam. Then she went to Canada to join an experimental college called Rochedale in Toronto.

"And then I was involved in helping all these draft dodgers and deserters, and for two or three years I was one of the adult figures in the counterculture. Rochedale was an eighteen-story high-rise hippie college. It was bootstrap-financed in such a way that it became the highly mortgaged property of those people who were members of Rochedale College—government financing piled onto private mortgages onto chicanery. It has been in the process of folding since shortly after it began. The building is now in receivership, and the last couple of hundred people are being shoveled out with shoehorns, because they've dug themselves in so tight, but the concept with which it began lasted I guess a year and a half or two years, at which point it had become rather than an attempt at variant educational structure, a cause and a large commune. However, the offshoots from it have permeated the city and various parts of Canada to such an extent that in certain ways it continues regardless—there is a farm group up in northern Ontario, and there's a theater group here, and people doing other things other places, all of which originated there, and came out of it as it became too complicated and difficult to do things there—so it either folded a year and a half after it started, or it is now folding, or it didn't fold at all."

Under new ownership after A. A. Wyn's death in 1968, Ace Books grew demoralized and overextended. The time came when the company was so deeply in debt that it could no longer borrow money to cover its current expenses. Signed contracts began to pile up on Wollheim's desk: he did not dare return them to the authors, because he knew there was no money to make the advance payments which were due on signing. One day he realized that a manuscript for which there was no valid contract had gone to the printer. "I knew the author," he told me, "and when I saw him a year or so later, I found out that during that summer he had three thousand dollars overdue him from Ace, and he was reduced to picking fruit for a living."

Wollheim had seen the end coming, and had been looking into the possibility of setting up his own publishing company. He had talked to New American Library about this, and had made tentative arrangements for them to be copublishers of a new company to be called DAW Books. Wollheim went through with these plans, and published his first four books in April 1972. NAL put up most of the capital for the new company; it provides office space and all services, distributes the books, and divides the profits with DAW, an arrangement Wollheim considers ideal.

At sixty-one Wollheim is relaxed and self-assured. In the modern living room of his house in Rego Park, where I talked to him and his wife Elsie twice in 1975, he seemed much more open and friendly than he had been when I knew him in the forties. In the old days there was always something Cassius-like, undernourished, about him; now he has gained just enough weight to make him seem no longer awkwardly proportioned.

After thirty years as a salaried editor, Wollheim is his own master. DAW Books is a small operation compared to Ace Books, and Wollheim can handle it without strain. He takes off a week now and then when he feels like it, travels to Europe three times a year. He still goes to science fiction conventions and to conventions of toy-soldier collectors, following an interest he has kept up all these years.

Under the coffee table as we talked was the Wollheims'

16-pound black and white tomcat, Big Daddy, so called because of all the black and white kittens in the neighborhood. Big Daddy was a street cat before they got him, Wollheim said. "We can't let him out much, because if he sees another tomcat, he goes straight for the throat or the balls."

Wollheim's instinct for intrigue, sharpened by his experiences in science fiction fandom, served him well in the highly competitive field of paperback publishing. His long effort has paid off at last: he is a publisher, a member of the bourgeoisie which he formerly blamed for the ills of mankind.

Isaac Asimov sat in my New York hotel room with his jacket off, reading from the pages of his diary. His voice was loud and jolly; sometimes, when he told me a well-worn anecdote, he laughed theatrically. Midway through the interview, his wife called: she had just had a message from the Asimovs' answering service that I had moved to another room, and she was afraid that Asimov, not knowing the new room number, would be wandering about helplessly.

Three or four of the other surviving Futurians might be justly described as famous, but Asimov is a celebrity. He has written nearly two hundred books; he appears on television, not merely on talk shows, but in tire commercials. He lives in Manhattan with his second wife, Janet Jeppson, a psychoanalyst.

I asked him what would have happened if his parents had not left Russia. He said, "I'll tell you exactly. If I'd stayed in Russia I would undoubtedly have received an education roughly equivalent to what I had here; I would undoubtedly have started writing in Russia; I might not have written science fiction, but I might have . . . and then, in 1941, I would have been killed in the war."

Asimov at fifty-six looks well nourished and cheerful; like Ray Bradbury, he has the buttery smile of one accustomed to praise. Under this and under his Sam Levenson comic manner, he is still vulnerable, still smarts at insults delivered thirty years ago. He is extraordinarily careful of other people's feelings, because his own are so easily wounded.

Columbia Publications, because of its low overhead, held out longer than the big pulp chains, but in 1960 it failed. "The distributor threw us out," Lowndes told me, "and the entire chain was killed off. I was mostly unemployed in 1960, but Don suggested I advertise in *Publishers Weekly*. I did, and got two replies: the first one came to nothing, and the second was from Louis Elson of Acme News—he was looking for an editor for *Exploring the Unknown*. And so I took that job, and of course it turned out to be a wonderful exercise in nostalgia in which I was reviving *Weird Tales* in my own way and some of the old science fiction magazines in *Famous Science Fiction*."

Like the Columbia magazines, these were marginal publications, poorly printed and not well distributed. In 1971 they went out of business, and Lowndes was offered a job as associate editor of *Sexology*. There he is today, where it all started, in the office of Gernsback Publications at 200 Park Avenue South, near East 17th Street. He lives in a tenement on a dark street in Hoboken, alone except for a mad cat named MacHeath. His railroad apartment is like something out of the forties: the kitchen is a dingy white horror, untouched since 1945; the other three rooms are painted kelly green or mandarin orange. On the walls of the front room are half a dozen citations and plaques; between the windows is an oil portrait of Lowndes, painted by the illustrator Kelly Freas twenty years ago.

Lowndes has changed more than any of the other Futurians since I last saw them: he is rounder and softer, a gentle white-haired old man. Like most of the Futurians, he seemed genuinely glad to see me; but more than this, I felt in him a loving acceptance that moved and touched me.

Sitting in his living room one fall evening in 1975, he told me about his experiences with psychotherapy and religion. "I was passionately interested in Reichian therapy at one time, and let me say that passion is past. It had to do with what Wilhelm Reich called the muscular armor. The physical thing was what worked on you, much like some other people who work on muscles; but Reich's theory was that your emotional problems would set up physical 'armoring' in various parts of your body, and these were locked into the emotional problems themselves; and if you could just unlock these tight spots in the body, then at the same time you could unlock the emotions and be released.

"It sounds like a lovely idea, and to a certain extent I found that it was true. I had tried talk therapy before then, the Horney type, and the trouble was I just couldn't talk. I just lay there, so scared of the whole business that I couldn't move. So after taking Reichian therapy, I could go into ordinary therapy and talk."

I knew that in the sixties he had become an Anglican and had taken a saint's name, signing himself Robert A. (for Augustine) W. Lowndes, and I asked him to talk about that.

"I was brought up as a Methodist," he said, "and I broke away from the church and became a Stalinist. When I became entirely fed up with Stalinism, and also fed up with liberalism, I started thinking about the church again. In 1955 I was seriously considering going down to the Roman Catholic church in Suffern for instruction, when I encountered Randall Garrett [a science fiction writer well known in the fifties], and he told

me I would find what I wanted in the Episcopal Church. And I
did find it there: I became an Anglican—high-church Episcopal. I was an Anglican from 1955 to '68 or '69. It was a slow
erosion, just like my dropping out of the Communist Party.
But it helped me through an immensely difficult period."

I asked him if he thought both religion and Communism
were crutches for him.

"Specific forms of religion, yes. But I do not consider
religion itself a crutch. I am not an atheist, and I'm not a
materialist. I am quite convinced that I, and you, Damon dear,
are entirely immortal—although not in these aching bodies,
thank God."

I noticed a copy of Jane Roberts' *Seth Speaks* on the coffee
table, and asked him what he thought of it. (*Seth Speaks* is a
book of spiritualist dialogs with a spook named Seth, spoken in
trance by Jane Roberts, the woman who went into trance at the
first meeting of the Five.)

"I'm reading it for the fourth time, and I haven't ex-
hausted it yet. I mean, that's stuff that I want to get into my
system. I would say that I am perhaps closer to spiritualism
than anything else. But I am just heretical enough to say, no, I
am not a spiritualist."

I married Kate Wilhelm in 1963, a year after my divorce from
Helen; we lived first in Milford, then in Fairdale, Kentucky;
Milford again; Treasure Island, Florida; Milford; Madeira
Beach, Florida; and finally Eugene, Oregon. During this
period I founded Science Fiction Writers of America (1965)
and the *Orbit* series of anthologies (1966).

After my marriage to Kate I had stopped seeing the Cohens, feeling that I wanted a clean break with all the friends
and quasi-friends Helen and I had accumulated. Kornbluth
was dead; Blish was living in New York, then in England;

Merril went off to England, then Canada. The only Futurian I saw at all frequently was Fred Pohl, who came to Conference weekends every other year or so, perhaps moved by the same lion-baiting spirit that had brought him to the Embassy years before.

My feelings toward Pohl had always been mixed; I admired and looked up to him as an older brother, but his kindnesses to me, although frequent, seemed Olympian. In his presence I felt a spontaneous affection for him which I think was reciprocated, but in correspondence and in print we always quarreled.

Pohl lives alone now in his big crumbling house in Red Bank, New Jersey. Some of the walls look a little naked, because his wife Carol took part of the furniture when she left in 1974, but the rooms are still full of huge flaking mirrors, massive sideboards, lamps, books, pictures. Pohl, like Wollheim, has gained a little weight since his thirties, just enough to make him look thin rather than gaunt. Two years before our interview he had had a Stalinoid mustache; the next year he had added a ratty beard; now he was clean-shaven again.

Pohl edited *Galaxy* magazine for ten years. When the magazine was sold in 1971 to Universal Publishing & Distributing Corp. (publishers of Beacon Books), Pohl resigned. In the fall of that year Ace offered him Wollheim's old job and he accepted, but found the situation there as intolerable as Wollheim had, and quit after eight months. In 1973 he became a consulting editor for Bantam Books, working in the office one day a week.

Since his last marriage and his last fulltime job ended, Pohl has had an exhilarating sense of freedom. He has been deliberately experimenting with life-styles, and with avocations such as folk-singing and cookery. His financial success as a writer and editor has liberated him, not only from wage servitude, as in Wollheim's case, but from every sort of dependence. In 1975 he finished two novels, lectured widely, served as president of Science Fiction Writers of America, and took his second trip behind the Iron Curtain under State Department auspices. Even he doesn't know what he will do next.

13

IN SOME UNDERGROUND WAY I THINK
HE DID KNOW—HAD ALWAYS KNOWN

What are we to make of the strain of catastrophic illness that runs through all these life histories? Michel's mother and Harry Dockweiler died of tuberculosis of the spine. Wilson's father was tubercular, and so was Walter Kubilius. Merril's father was stricken by encephalitis, which contributed to his suicide, in an epidemic that followed the influenza epidemic of 1918-19 in which Lowndes's mother died. Wollheim was paralyzed by polio, which also followed in the train of the influenza epidemic. (Later, so was Kidd.) Michel was paralyzed by diphtheria toxin, then suffered from osteomyelitis; and so on. The sample is so small that all this can be dismissed, if you like, as coincidence.

What does seem clear is that there was something in the early lives of nearly all the published writers in the group that isolated them from their contemporaries. Blish, Pohl, Michel, Merril, and I were only children. Pohl, Blish, Wilson,

Lowndes, Merril and Michel lost one parent each in childhood, by death or divorce. Wilson skipped three grades in grammar school. Asimov's time was so taken up by his work in the candy store, his education and his writing that there was not much left over for normal relationships with other young people. None of these things were true of me, but I suffered from general constitutional weakness—I looked like the 97-pound weakling in the body-building ads of the thirties.

Beyond all this, it may be argued that we were isolated in childhood merely because we were brighter and more talented than others. Unfortunately, there is no way to tell how much variation of this kind is due to early environment and how much is genetic. As for creativity, nobody knows what it is or how to measure it.

My quasi-belief is that what we call creativity is the survival instinct expressing itself in unorthodox ways. Most of the writers I know have used their art to escape from the locked rooms of intolerable circumstances. In one study which compared "general writers," artists, and science fiction writers, the s.f. writers scored a little higher than the other two groups in nearly everything from intelligence to dominance, and remarkably higher in one thing—"adventurous cyclothymia": s.f. writers 25.4 (25.4% higher than the general population), general writers 5.7, artists 4.7. What this appears to mean is that s.f. writers, confronted with desperate problems, may mope, but are much more likely to break out by some dazzling improvisation; they have what Arthur Koestler calls "the coward's courage."

I once had a life-class instructor who maintained that anybody could be taught to draw, and I think to a limited extent the same is true of writing: that is, any reasonably intelligent and educated person can be taught to write, up to the limit of what is understandable about writing and maybe a little beyond it. But the most important things about writing are not understandable.

As a child I had the idea that I could learn to fly by jumping, then jumping again before I had time to fall back to earth. I never succeeded in this, but it seems to me now that when someone turns himself from a mediocre writer into a good one, it is by exactly this process. Somehow we must reach beyond what we know, and do what we can't do; and I think it's the fear of psychic death that drives us to attempt this impossible thing.

Most of the Futurian writers perceived themselves as underdogs, and had strong feelings of resentment toward those they believed were keeping them down, but there was an unanalyzed distinction between Wollheim, for instance, who believed he was capable and would eventually become a top dog, and Michel, who needed to feel snubbed. Wollheim's need was for mastery, Michel's for injustice.

"I had this discussion with my shrink," said Pohl, "talking about my self-image, and he asked what I thought of myself, and I said, 'Well, I used to hang around with a bunch of pretty bright kids.' There was more to the conversation, but I guess somebody had shown me a picture of the Futurians, and I was trying to see if there was any way you could tell by looking at them which ones were going to amount to something and which ones were going to die drunk."

I have tried to remember what it could have been that I saw in Michel that made me call him self-destructive. I think I had a sense that he was throwing away opportunities, alienating friends, out of some deep need for failure and death. Pohl's remark about those who were going to die drunk was made before he could have known what happened to Michel, but in some underground way I think he did know—had always known.

Writers are pattern makers. Sometimes the patterns they make survive them. Cyril Kornbluth died in 1958, but some of his novels and stories have been reprinted and are alive. Of all the words John Michel wrote, only those quoted in this book are in print.

Writers, intent on the patterns they make, sometimes are slow to realize that their own lives are also patterns. John Michel's life had an inevitable trajectory; it was good art. Harry Dockweiler's life and death were bad art.

The special conditions that created the Futurians have not recurred, and there has never been another group like it, although s.f. fans and aspiring writers have shared housing in other times and places. One of these conditions was poverty: as soon as the Futurians began to make a little money, the group began to dissolve. Another was political intransigence, arising partly out of the Futurians' sense of rejection by the system. Still another was the early growth of science fiction magazines, which offered opportunities to young writers and editors at a time when there were few other opportunities.

Under our hostilities and irritations there was always a strong affection that held the Futurians together. I think we were all lucky to have had that, and to have had each other. There are no second chances. In Kornbluth's words (but he spoke for all of us, not just for the Futurians):

> *We do not come again.*
> *We do not come. Ever again.*

APPENDIX

Ballad for Futurians
Words by Cyril Kornbluth and Chester Cohen (to the tune of
"Ballad for Americans")

In thirty-eight, when I was red,
And Gernsback rumbled overhead,
Dirty Will couldn't sleep in his bed,
   And on that stormy morn
   The CPASF was born!
Then the Nycon came with a great big roar,
And Willy loused as he had before:
And the valiant six went around and round
To see where justice could be found:
But to fascist tactics Will was bound.
Nobody who was anybody believed it;
Morojo and Ackerman, they doubted it.

But Philly believed it, and Newark believed it too.
And you know what they are.
  They're just a bunch of dirty lousy bastards,
  *Pimps and perverts, pfumpfs and fooches,**
  Sodomites and syphilitics—
  Goons and wacks and jerks and lots more—
  They sure are the whole turd!
The Futurians grew in peace and war,
And they're growing stronger than before.
  High as our speeches, low as our motives,
  Vile as the people who govern us!
But we have always believed it
And we believe it now.
And you know who we are:
  The SF world!

---

*The Futurians explained to me that a pfumpf is someone who farts in the bathtub and bites the bubbles as they come up; a fooch is a man who smells girls' bicycle seats in summer.

CRY in the NIGHT

Cyril Kornbluth

James Blish
Opus 5, No. 1

Andantino con rubato

Cry in the night, gulls, inside her skull, behind her green eyes,

is the lean, lu-na-tic Inqui-si-tion.

Cry in the night; re-mem-ber, she hath no fear, though her

heart burst a-sun-der.

S.C way e, 1944

for
Larry Shaw

INDEX